GreatBooks
Roundtable

Level 3

GreatBooks
Roundtable

Level 3

GreatBooks
Foundation

Copyright © 2010 by The Great Books Foundation
Chicago, Illinois
All rights reserved
ISBN 978-1-933147-55-0

First Printing
2 4 6 8 9 7 5 3 1
Printed in the United States of America

Library of Congress Cataloging-in-Publication Data

Great books roundtable. Level 3.
   p. cm.
  ISBN 978-1-933147-55-0 (alk. paper)
  1. Reading (Middle school)–United States. 2. Reading comprehension–
United States. 3. Children–Books and reading–United States. I. Great
Books Foundation (U.S.)
LB1632.G74 2010c
372.47–dc22

2009027497

Published and distributed by

THE GREAT BOOKS FOUNDATION
A nonprofit educational organization

35 East Wacker Drive, Suite 400

Chicago, IL 60601

www.greatbooks.org

CONTENTS

PREFACE

Welcome to Great Books Roundtable™! In this reading and discussion program, you will be using a learning method called **Shared Inquiry.**™ In Shared Inquiry, you develop your own **interpretation** of what you read.

Authors do not usually tell us exactly how the parts of a work of literature are connected or spell out why everything in a story happens.

But in good writing, everything fits together and is there for a reason. The parts of the text connect and support each other as the parts of a building do.

Because the parts of a good piece of writing are connected, they help explain one another. Good authors put into their writing the things a reader must know to understand what is happening and why. As you figure out for yourself why the things an author puts in a text are there, you are interpreting what you read. To **interpret** a text is to explain its meaning—what happens in it, and why, and what it is about. Many texts, like those in Great Books programs, support more than one interpretation. When you interpret a text, you are actively seeking out its meaning by asking and exploring questions.

HOW SHARED INQUIRY WORKS

In Shared Inquiry, you read literature that makes you **think and ask questions**.

After reading or listening to the story, poem, or essay, everyone in the group shares questions about it. Some questions can be answered right away. Others will be saved for discussion or other activities.

Everyone then rereads the text and makes notes. Afterward, you all compare your reactions to parts of the text.

You will develop your interpretation of a text most fully in **Shared Inquiry discussion**. During discussion, everyone thinks about the meaning of the text in depth. People sit so everyone can see all the members of the group, and the leader starts discussion with an **interpretive question**—a question that has more than one good answer that can be supported with evidence from the text.

What Shared Inquiry Discussion Looks Like

In a Shared Inquiry discussion, the leader isn't looking for the "right answer." Rather, the leader starts with a question that has more than one good answer based on the text and wants to hear ideas about it.

The leader asks questions to help everyone think more deeply.

In addition to sharing your ideas, you can agree or disagree with someone or ask him a question about his comment.

You can also ask someone to explain her idea a bit more.

At the end of discussion, people will have different answers to the opening question, but everyone will have a better understanding of the text and the evidence for his or her answer. You may change your answer because of what you hear in discussion or hear new evidence to support your original answer.

SHARED INQUIRY DISCUSSION: FIVE GUIDELINES

People of all ages, from kindergartners to adults, participate in Shared Inquiry discussion groups. All participants follow these five guidelines, which help everyone share ideas about the text and learn from one another.

 Read the text twice before participating in the discussion.

 Discuss only the text that everyone has read.

3 Support your ideas with evidence from the text.

4 Listen to other participants, respond to them directly, and ask them questions.

5 Expect the leader to only ask questions, rather than offer opinions or answers.

SHARED INQUIRY DISCUSSION ETIQUETTE

DO

Let other people
talk, and listen to
what they say.

DON'T

Talk over people
and keep others
from speaking.

DO

Speak up! You may
have an idea no one else
has thought of.

DON'T

Be afraid to
share your ideas.

DO

Be willing to think
about new ideas.
Disagree politely.

DON'T

Take it personally
when someone disagrees
with your idea.

DO

Pay attention—it shows
respect for the members
of your group.

DON'T

Distract people or act
as if their ideas aren't
worth hearing.

TYPES OF QUESTIONS

Asking yourself questions is the most important thing you can do while you are reading. When you ask questions, you are helping yourself organize your thoughts about what in the text is interesting, confusing, surprising, shocking, funny, familiar, or sad. You are also preparing to explore the text more deeply the next time you read it. Below are different types of questions you might ask while reading. Notice that it's not always important—or even possible—to answer questions right away.

Factual questions can usually be answered after one thorough reading. The text provides information for a single correct answer.

EXAMPLES: *Where is Mourad keeping the horse?* ("The Summer of the Beautiful White Horse")
Is Miss Strangeworth the anonymous letter writer? ("The Possibility of Evil")
Why does Sucker live with the narrator and his family? ("Sucker")

Background questions must be answered by information outside the text. They might be questions about the historical period in which the text is set, or questions about a character's culture. Sources that can help answer these questions include an encyclopedia, a textbook, the Internet, or a teacher who knows the subject.

EXAMPLES: *Where is Armenia?* ("The Summer of the Beautiful White Horse")
Who is Ethan Allen? ("The Possibility of Evil")
What type of reading is Popular Mechanics? ("Sucker")

Evaluative questions go beyond the text and call for the reader's personal opinions. Such questions often ask for a judgment of events or a character's actions.

EXAMPLES: *Should Mourad be punished for taking the horse?*
("The Summer of the Beautiful White Horse")
What is the best way to respond to someone who spreads rumors? ("The Possibility of Evil")
Is excluding someone from a group ever appropriate?
("Fellowship")

Speculative questions, like background questions, ask about information that exists outside the text, but readers must guess at or invent the answer using their imagination.

EXAMPLES: *Will Aram and Mourad take the horse again?*
("The Summer of the Beautiful White Horse")
Does Miss Ferenczi have a family? ("Gryphon")
Is the narrator ever going to be able to make up with Sucker? ("Sucker")

Interpretive questions, which get at the text's deeper meaning and themes, are the kind of questions that will be addressed in Shared Inquiry discussion. They have more than one good answer that can be supported with evidence from the text.

EXAMPLES: *Why doesn't John Byro accuse the boys of stealing his horse?*
("The Summer of the Beautiful White Horse")
Why does Tommy defend Miss Ferenczi? ("Gryphon")
According to the text, what is a "friend"? ("Fellowship")

READING STRATEGIES

Strong readers use certain strategies to help them understand what they read. If you are reading a confusing or puzzling passage, stop and try to figure out which of the reading strategies listed below might help you understand it more clearly. To help you keep track of which strategy you are using, mark your text in the margins with the letters or symbols suggested below:

R   **REREADING**   Go back and reread when you are reading something that is difficult to understand, or when you realize that you haven't been focusing on what you are reading.

?   **ASKING QUESTIONS**   Ask a question about something in the text you find puzzling or confusing.

C   **MAKING CONNECTIONS**   Connect or compare something that happens in the text with something you have experienced or learned yourself.

V   **VISUALIZING**   Create a picture in your head of what is going on in the text. Imagine sights, smells, sounds, and feelings.

!   **NOTING STRONG REACTIONS**   Stop and think about something in the text that causes you to feel a strong reaction (positive *or* negative).

I   **MAKING INFERENCES**   Combine clues in the text with your own ideas to fill in "missing pieces" of the text—places where the author doesn't directly tell you what's going on, but gives you hints by using description, dialogue, or other writing devices.

P   **PREDICTING**   Pause while reading and make a guess, based on your own ideas and the clues in the text, about what might happen next.

If you practice all these strategies, you will eventually begin to use several at a time automatically as you read. Using different comprehension strategies while reading, called *synthesizing*, is how a good reader comes to understand a complex text.

QUICK KEY to Marking Your Text	
R = Rereading	! = Noting strong reactions
? = Asking questions	I = Making inferences
C = Making connections	P = Predicting
V = Visualizing	

FOLLOW-UP QUESTIONS

In Shared Inquiry discussion, the leader isn't the only person who can ask questions. You can respond to your classmates directly by asking them questions yourself. These kinds of questions are called **follow-up questions** because they are useful to ask right after you hear an idea and want to find out more about it. Examples of follow-up questions include:

- Can you say more about what you mean?
- When you say the character is [word or phrase], what do you mean?
- When you say [word or phrase], what do you mean?
- What happened that gave you that idea?
- What part of the story supports your idea?
- What do you think about this other part?
- Are you agreeing with Maya's answer?
- Why do you agree with what William said?
- So how does your idea fit with Ethan's idea?

Remember: A follow-up question is a compliment. When you ask a follow-up question, you are showing that you are listening and thinking about what others are saying. When someone asks you a follow-up question, that person is displaying interest in your idea.

The Summer of the Beautiful White Horse

William Saroyan

One day back there in the good old days when I was nine and the world was full of every imaginable kind of magnificence, and life was still a delightful and mysterious dream, my cousin Mourad, who was considered crazy by everybody who knew him except me, came to my house at four in the morning and woke me up by tapping on the window of my room.

Aram, he said.

I jumped out of bed and looked out the window.

I couldn't believe what I saw.

It wasn't morning yet, but it was summer and with daybreak not many minutes around the corner of the world it was light enough for me to know I wasn't dreaming.

My cousin Mourad was sitting on a beautiful white horse.

I stuck my head out of the window and rubbed my eyes.

Yes, he said in Armenian. It's a horse. You're not dreaming. Make it quick if you want to ride.

I knew my cousin Mourad enjoyed being alive more than anybody else who had ever fallen into the world by mistake, but this was more than even I could believe.

In the first place, my earliest memories had been memories of horses and my first longings had been longings to ride.

This was the wonderful part.

In the second place, we were poor.

This was the part that wouldn't permit me to believe what I saw.

We were poor. We had no money. Our whole tribe was poverty-stricken. Every branch of the Garoghlanian family was living in the most amazing and comical poverty in the world. Nobody could understand where we ever got money enough to keep us with food in our bellies, not even the old men of the family. Most important of all, though, we were famous for our honesty. We had been famous for our honesty for something like eleven centuries, even when we had been the wealthiest family in what we liked to think was the world. We were proud first, honest next, and after that we believed in right and wrong. None of us would take advantage of anybody in the world, let alone steal.

Consequently, even though I could *see* the horse, so magnificent; even though I could *smell* it, so lovely; even though I could *hear* it breathing, so exciting; I couldn't *believe* the horse had anything to do with my cousin Mourad or with me or with any of the other members of our family, asleep or awake, because I *knew* my cousin Mourad couldn't have *bought* the horse, and if he couldn't have bought it he must have *stolen* it, and I refused to believe he had stolen it.

No member of the Garoghlanian family could be any kind of a thief, let alone a horse thief.

I stared first at my cousin and then at the horse. There was a pious stillness and humor in each of them which on the one hand delighted me and on the other frightened me.

Mourad, I said, where did you steal this horse?

Leap out of the window, he said, if you want to ride.

It was true, then. He *had* stolen the horse. There was no question about it. He had come to invite me to ride or not, as I chose.

Well, it seemed to me stealing a horse for a ride was not the same thing as stealing something else, such as money. For all I knew, maybe it wasn't stealing at all. If you were crazy about horses the way my cousin Mourad and I were, it wasn't stealing. It wouldn't become stealing until we offered to sell the horse, which of course I knew we would never do.

Let me put on some clothes, I said.

All right, he said, but hurry.

I leaped into my clothes.

I jumped down to the yard from the window and leaped up onto the horse behind my cousin Mourad.

That year we lived at the edge of town, on Walnut Avenue. Behind our house was the country: vineyards, orchards, irrigation ditches, and country roads. In less than three minutes we were on Olive Avenue, and then the horse began to trot. The air was new and lovely to breathe. The feel of the horse running was wonderful. My cousin Mourad, who was considered one of the craziest members of our family, began to sing. I mean, he began to roar.

Every family has a crazy streak in it somewhere, and my cousin Mourad was considered the natural inheritor of the crazy streak in our tribe. Before him was our uncle Khosrove, an enormous man with a powerful head of black hair and the largest mustache in the San Joaquin Valley, a man so furious in

3

temper, so irritable, so impatient that he stopped anyone from talking by roaring, *It is no harm; pay no attention to it.*

That was all, no matter what anybody happened to be talking about. Once it was his own son Arak running eight blocks to the barber shop where his father was having his mustache trimmed to tell him their house was on fire. This man Khosrove sat up in the chair and roared, It is no harm; pay no attention to it. The barber said, But the boy says your house is on fire. So Khosrove roared, Enough, it is no harm, I say.

My cousin Mourad was considered the descendant of this man, although Mourad's father was Zorab, who was practical and nothing else. That's how it was in our tribe. A man could be the father of his son's flesh, but that did not mean that he was also the father of his spirit. The distribution of the various kinds of spirit of our tribe had been from the beginning capricious and vagrant.

We rode and my cousin Mourad sang. For all anybody knew we were still in the old country where, at least according to some of our neighbors, we belonged. We let the horse run as long as it felt like running.

At last my cousin Mourad said, Get down. I want to ride alone.

Will you let me ride alone?

That is up to the horse.

The *horse* will let me ride.

We shall see. Don't forget that I have a way with a horse.

Well, any way you have with a horse, I have also.

For the sake of your safety, he said, let us hope so. Get down.

All right, I said, but remember you've got to let me try to ride alone.

I got down and my cousin Mourad kicked his heels into the horse and shouted, *Vazire*, run. The horse stood on its hind legs, snorted, and burst into a fury of speed that was the loveliest thing I had ever seen. My cousin Mourad raced the horse across a field of dry grass to an irrigation ditch, crossed the ditch on the horse, and five minutes later came back, dripping wet.

The sun was coming up, and so everything had bright light upon it, especially the horse.

Now it's my turn to ride, I said.

My cousin Mourad got off the horse.

Ride, he said.

I leaped to the back of the horse and for a moment knew the awfulest fear imaginable. The horse did not move.

Kick into his muscles, my cousin Mourad said. What are you waiting for? We've got to take him back before everybody in the world is up and about.

I kicked into the muscles of the horse. Once again it reared and snorted. Then it began to run. I didn't know what to do. Instead of running across the field to the irrigation ditch the horse ran down the road to the vineyard of Dikran Halabian where it began to leap over vines. The horse leaped over seven vines before I fell. Then it ran away.

My cousin Mourad came running down the road.

I'm not worried about you, he shouted. We've got to get that horse. You go this way and I'll go this way. If you come upon him, be kindly. I'll be near.

I ran down the road and my cousin Mourad ran across the field toward the irrigation ditch.

It took him half an hour to find the horse and bring him back.

All right, he said, jump on. The whole world is awake now.

What will we do? I said.

Well, he said, we'll either take him back or hide him until tomorrow morning.

He didn't sound worried and I knew he'd hide him and not take him back. Not for a while, at any rate.

Where will we hide him?

I know a place.

How long ago did you steal this horse? I said.

It suddenly dawned on me that he had been taking these early morning rides for some time and had come for me this morning only because he knew how much I longed to ride.

Who said anything about stealing a horse?

Anyhow, how long ago did you begin riding every morning?

Not until this morning.

Are you telling the truth?

Of course not, he said, but if we are found out, that's what you're to say. I don't want both of us to be liars. All you know is that we started riding this morning.

All right, I said.

He walked the horse quietly to the barn of a deserted vineyard which at one time had been the pride of a farmer named Vahan Fetvajian. There were some oats and dry alfalfa in the barn.

We began walking home.

It wasn't easy, he said, to get the horse to behave so nicely. At first it wanted to run wild, but, as I've told you, I have a way with a horse. I can get it to want to do anything *I* want it to do. Horses understand me.

How do you do it? I said.

I have an understanding with a horse.

Yes, but what kind of an understanding?

A simple and honest one.

Well, I wish I knew how to reach an understanding like that with a horse.

You're still a small boy, he said. When you get to be thirteen you'll know how to do it.

I went home and ate a hearty breakfast.

That afternoon my uncle Khosrove came to our house for coffee and cigarettes. He sat in the parlor, sipping and smoking and remembering the old country. Then another visitor arrived, a farmer named John Byro, an Assyrian who, out of loneliness, had learned to speak Armenian. My mother brought the lonely visitor coffee and tobacco and he rolled a cigarette and sipped and smoked, and then at last, sighing sadly, he said, My white horse which was stolen last month is still gone. I cannot understand it.

My uncle Khosrove became very irritated and shouted, It's no harm. What is the loss of a horse? Haven't we all lost the homeland? What is this crying over a horse?

That may be all right for you, a city dweller, to say, but what about my surrey? What good is a surrey without a horse?

Pay no attention to it, my uncle Khosrove roared.

I walked ten miles to get here.

You have legs.

My left leg pains me.

Pay no attention to it.

That horse cost me sixty dollars, John Byro said.

I spit on money, my uncle Khosrove said.

He got up and stalked out of the house, slamming the screen door.

My mother explained.

He has a gentle heart, she said. It is simply that he is homesick and such a large man.

The farmer went away and I ran over to my cousin Mourad's house.

He was sitting under a peach tree, repairing the hurt wing of a young robin which could not fly. He was talking to the bird.

What is it? he said.

The farmer, John Byro. He visited our house. He wants his horse. You've had it a month. I want you to promise not to take it back until I learn to ride.

It will take you a *year* to learn to ride.

We could keep the horse a year.

My cousin Mourad leaped to his feet.

What? he roared. Are you inviting a member of the Garoghlanian family to steal? The horse must go back to its true owner.

When?

In six months at the latest.

He threw the bird into the air. The bird tried hard, almost fell twice, but at last flew away, high and straight.

Early every morning for two weeks my cousin Mourad and I took the horse out of the barn of the deserted vineyard where we were hiding it and rode it, and every morning the horse, when it was my turn to ride alone, leaped over grapevines and small trees and threw me and ran away. Nevertheless, I hoped in time to learn to ride the way my cousin Mourad rode.

One morning on our way to Vahan Fetvajian's deserted vineyard we ran into the farmer John Byro who was on his way to town.

Let me do the talking, my cousin Mourad said. I have a way with farmers.

Good morning, John Byro, my cousin Mourad said to the farmer.

The farmer studied the horse eagerly.

Good morning, sons of my friends, he said. What is the name of your horse?

My Heart, my cousin Mourad said in Armenian.

A lovely name for a lovely horse. I could swear it is the horse that was stolen from me many weeks ago. May I look into its mouth?

Of course, Mourad said.

The farmer looked into the mouth of the horse.

Tooth for tooth, he said. I would swear it *is* my horse if I didn't know your parents. The fame of your family for honesty is well known to me. Yet the horse is the twin of my horse. A suspicious man would believe his eyes instead of his heart. Good day, my young friends.

Good day, John Byro, my cousin Mourad said.

Early the following morning we took the horse to John Byro's vineyard and put it in the barn. The dogs followed us around without making a sound.

The dogs, I whispered to my cousin Mourad. I thought they would bark.

They would at somebody else, he said. I have a way with dogs.

My cousin Mourad put his arms around the horse, pressed his nose into the horse's nose, patted it, and then we went away.

That afternoon John Byro came to our house in his surrey and showed my mother the horse that had been stolen and returned.

I do not know what to think, he said. The horse is stronger than ever. Better-tempered, too. I thank God.

My uncle Khosrove, who was out of sight in the parlor, suddenly shouted. Quiet, man, quiet. Your horse has been returned. Pay no attention to it.

SUCKER

Carson McCullers

It was always like I had a room to myself. Sucker slept in my bed with me but that didn't interfere with anything. The room was mine and I used it as I wanted to. Once I remember sawing a trap door in the floor. Last year when I was a sophomore in high school I tacked on my wall some pictures of girls from magazines and one of them was just in her underwear. My mother never bothered me because she had the younger kids to look after. And Sucker thought anything I did was always swell.

Whenever I would bring any of my friends back to my room all I had to do was just glance once at Sucker and he would get up from whatever he was busy with and maybe half smile at me, and leave without saying a word. He never brought kids back there. He's twelve, four years younger than I am, and he always knew without me even telling him that I didn't want kids that age meddling with my things.

Half the time I used to forget that Sucker isn't my brother. He's my first cousin but practically ever since I remember he's been in our family. You see his folks were killed in a wreck when he was a baby. To me and my kid sisters he was like our brother.

Sucker used to always remember and believe every word I said. That's how he got his nickname. Once a couple of years ago I told him that if he'd jump off our garage with an umbrella it would act as a parachute and he wouldn't fall hard. He did it and busted his knee. That's just one instance. And the funny thing was that no matter how many times he got fooled he would still believe me. Not that he was dumb in other ways—it was just the way he acted with me. He would look at everything I did and quietly take it in.

There is one thing I have learned, but it makes me feel guilty and is hard to figure out. If a person admires you a lot you despise him and don't care—and it is the person who doesn't notice you that you are apt to admire. This is not easy to realize. Maybelle Watts, this senior at school, acted like she was the Queen of Sheba and even humiliated me. Yet at this same time I would have done anything in the world to get her attentions. All I could think about day and night was Maybelle until I was nearly crazy. When Sucker was a little kid and on up until the time he was twelve I guess I treated him as bad as Maybelle did me.

Now that Sucker has changed so much it is a little hard to remember him as he used to be. I never imagined anything would suddenly happen that would make us both very different. I never knew that in order to get what has happened straight in my mind I would want to think back on him as he used to be and compare and try to get things settled. If I could have seen ahead maybe I would have acted different.

I never noticed him much or thought about him and when you consider how long we have had the same room together it is funny the few things I remember. He used to talk to himself a lot when he'd think he was alone—all about him fighting gangsters and being on ranches and that sort of kids' stuff. He'd get in the bathroom and stay as long as an hour and sometimes his voice would go up high and excited and you could hear him all over the house. Usually, though, he was very quiet. He didn't have many boys in the neighborhood to buddy with and his face had the look of a kid who is watching a game and waiting to be asked to play. He didn't mind wearing the sweaters and coats that I outgrew, even if the sleeves did flop down too big and make his wrists look as thin and white as a little girl's. That is how I remember him—getting a little bigger every year but still being the same. That was Sucker up until a few months ago when all this trouble began.

Maybelle was somehow mixed up in what happened so I guess I ought to start with her. Until I knew her I hadn't given much time to girls. Last fall she sat next to me in General Science class and that was when I first began to notice her. Her hair is the brightest yellow I ever saw and occasionally she will wear it set into curls with some sort of gluey stuff. Her fingernails are pointed and manicured and painted a shiny red. All during class I used to watch Maybelle, nearly all the time except when I thought she was going to look my way or when the teacher called on me. I couldn't keep my eyes off her hands, for one thing. They are very little and white except for that red stuff, and when she would turn the pages of her book she always licked her thumb and held out her little finger and turned very slowly. It is impossible to describe Maybelle. All the boys are crazy about her but she didn't even notice me. For one thing she's almost two years older than I am. Between periods I used to try and pass very close to her in the halls but she would hardly ever smile at me. All I could do was sit and look at her in

13

class—and sometimes it was like the whole room could hear my heart beating and I wanted to holler or light out and run for hell.

At night, in bed, I would imagine about Maybelle. Often this would keep me from sleeping until as late as one or two o'clock. Sometimes Sucker would wake up and ask me why I couldn't get settled and I'd tell him to hush his mouth. I suppose I was mean to him lots of times. I guess I wanted to ignore somebody like Maybelle did me. You could always tell by Sucker's face when his feelings were hurt. I don't remember all the ugly remarks I must have made because even when I was saying them my mind was on Maybelle.

That went on for nearly three months and then somehow she began to change. In the halls she would speak to me and every morning she copied my homework. At lunchtime once I danced with her in the gym. One afternoon I got up nerve and went around to her house with a carton of cigarettes. I knew she smoked in the girls' basement and sometimes outside of school—and I didn't want to take her candy because I think that's been run into the ground. She was very nice and it seemed to me everything was going to change.

It was that night when this trouble really started. I had come into my room late and Sucker was already asleep. I felt too happy and keyed up to get in a comfortable position and I was awake thinking about Maybelle a long time. Then I dreamed about her and it seemed I kissed her. It was a surprise to wake up and see the dark. I lay still and a little while passed before I could come to and understand where I was. The house was quiet and it was a very dark night.

Sucker's voice was a shock to me. "Pete? . . ."

I didn't answer anything or even move.

"You do like me as much as if I was your own brother, don't you Pete?"

14

I couldn't get over the surprise of everything and it was like this was the real dream instead of the other.

"You have liked me all the time like I was your own brother, haven't you?"

"Sure," I said.

Then I got up for a few minutes. It was cold and I was glad to come back to bed. Sucker hung on to my back. He felt little and warm and I could feel his warm breathing on my shoulder.

"No matter what you did I always knew you liked me."

I was wide awake and my mind seemed mixed up in a strange way. There was this happiness about Maybelle and all that—but at the same time something about Sucker and his voice when he said these things made me take notice. Anyway I guess you understand people better when you are happy than when something is worrying you. It was like I had never really thought about Sucker until then. I felt I had always been mean to him. One night a few weeks before I had heard him crying in the dark. He said he had lost a boy's BB gun and was scared to let anybody know. He wanted me to tell him what to do. I was sleepy and tried to make him hush and when he wouldn't I kicked at him. That was just one of the things I remembered. It seemed to me he had always been a lonesome kid. I felt bad.

There is something about a dark cold night that makes you feel close to someone you're sleeping with. When you talk together it is like you are the only people awake in the town.

"You're a swell kid, Sucker," I said.

It seemed to me suddenly that I did like him more than anybody else I knew—more than any other boy, more than my sisters, more in a certain way even than Maybelle. I felt good all over and it was like when they play sad music in the movies. I wanted to show Sucker how much I really thought of him and make up for the way I had always treated him.

15

We talked for a good while that night. His voice was fast and it was like he had been saving up these things to tell me for a long time. He mentioned that he was going to try to build a canoe and that the kids down the block wouldn't let him in on their football team and I don't know what all. I talked some too and it was a good feeling to think of him taking in everything I said so seriously. I even spoke of Maybelle a little, only I made out like it was her who had been running after me all this time. He asked questions about high school and so forth. His voice was excited and he kept on talking fast like he could never get the words out in time. When I went to sleep he was still talking and I could still feel his breathing on my shoulder, warm and close.

During the next couple of weeks I saw a lot of Maybelle. She acted as though she really cared for me a little. Half the time I felt so good I hardly knew what to do with myself.

But I didn't forget about Sucker. There were a lot of old things in my bureau drawer I'd been saving—boxing gloves and Tom Swift books and second-rate fishing tackle. All this I turned over to him. We had some more talks together and it was really like I was knowing him for the first time. When there was a long cut on his cheek I knew he had been monkeying around with this new first razor set of mine, but I didn't say anything. His face seemed different now. He used to look timid and sort of like he was afraid of a whack over the head. That expression was gone. His face, with those wide-open eyes and his ears sticking out and his mouth never quite shut, had the look of a person who is surprised and expecting something swell.

Once I started to point him out to Maybelle and tell her he was my kid brother. It was an afternoon when a murder mystery was on at the movie. I had earned a dollar working for my dad and I gave Sucker a quarter to go and get candy and so forth. With the rest I took Maybelle. We were sitting near the back and I saw Sucker come in. He began to stare at the screen the minute he stepped past the ticket man and he stumbled down the aisle without noticing where he was going. I started to punch Maybelle but couldn't quite make up my mind. Sucker looked a little silly—walking like a drunk with his eyes glued to the movie. He was wiping his reading glasses on his shirttail and his knickers flopped down. He went on until he got to the first few rows where the kids usually sit. I never did punch Maybelle. But I got to thinking it was good to have both of them at the movie with the money I earned.

I guess things went on like this for about a month or six weeks. I felt so good I couldn't settle down to study or put my mind on anything. I wanted to be friendly with everybody. There were times when I just had to talk to some person. And usually that would be Sucker. He felt as good as I did. Once he said: "Pete, I am gladder that you are like my brother than anything else in the world."

Then something happened between Maybelle and me. I never have figured out just what it was. Girls like her are hard to understand. She began to act different toward me. At first I wouldn't let myself believe this and tried to think it was just my imagination. She didn't act glad to see me anymore. Often she went out riding with this fellow on the football team who owns this yellow roadster. The car was the color of her hair and after school she would ride off with him, laughing and looking into his face. I couldn't think of anything to do about it and she was on my mind all day and night. When I did get a chance to go out with her she was snippy and didn't seem to notice me. This

17

made me feel like something was the matter—I would worry about my shoes clopping too loud on the floor, or the fly of my pants, or the bumps on my chin. Sometimes when Maybelle was around, a devil would get into me and I'd hold my face stiff and call grown men by their last names without the Mister and say rough things. In the night I would wonder what made me do all this until I was too tired for sleep.

At first I was so worried I just forgot about Sucker. Then later he began to get on my nerves. He was always hanging around until I would get back from high school, always looking like he had something to say to me or wanted me to tell him. He made me a magazine rack in his Manual Training class and one week he saved his lunch money and bought me three packs of cigarettes. He couldn't seem to take it in that I had things on my mind and didn't want to fool with him. Every afternoon it would be the same—him in my room with this waiting expression on his face. Then I wouldn't say anything or I'd maybe answer him rough-like and he would finally go on out.

I can't divide that time up and say this happened one day and that the next. For one thing I was so mixed up the weeks just slid along into each other and I felt like hell and didn't care. Nothing definite was said or done. Maybelle still rode around with this fellow in his yellow roadster and sometimes she would smile at me and sometimes not. Every afternoon I went from one place to another where I thought she would be. Either she would act almost nice and I would begin thinking how things would finally clear up and she would care for me—or else she'd behave so that if she hadn't been a girl I'd have wanted to grab her by that white little neck and choke her. The more ashamed I felt for making a fool of myself the more I ran after her.

18

Sucker kept getting on my nerves more and more. He would look at me as though he sort of blamed me for something, but at the same time knew that it wouldn't last long. He was growing fast and for some reason began to stutter when he talked. Sometimes he had nightmares or would throw up his breakfast. Mom got him a bottle of cod-liver oil.

Then the finish came between Maybelle and me. I met her going to the drugstore and asked for a date. When she said no I remarked something sarcastic. She told me she was sick and tired of my being around and that she had never cared a rap about me. She said all that. I just stood there and didn't answer anything. I walked home very slowly.

For several afternoons I stayed in my room by myself. I didn't want to go anywhere or talk to anyone. When Sucker would come in and look at me sort of funny I'd yell at him to get out. I didn't want to think of Maybelle and I sat at my desk reading *Popular Mechanics* or whittling at a toothbrush rack I was making. It seemed to me I was putting that girl out of my mind pretty well.

But you can't help what happens to you at night. That is what made things how they are now.

You see a few nights after Maybelle said those words to me I dreamed about her again. It was like that first time and I was squeezing Sucker's arm so tight I woke him up. He reached for my hand.

"Pete, what's the matter with you?"

All of a sudden I felt so mad my throat choked—at myself and the dream and Maybelle and Sucker and every single person I knew. I remembered all the times Maybelle had humiliated me and everything bad that had ever happened. It seemed to me for a second that nobody would ever like me but a sap like Sucker.

"Why is it we aren't buddies like we were before? Why—?"

"Shut your damn trap!" I threw off the cover and got up and turned on the light. He sat in the middle of the bed, his eyes blinking and scared.

There was something in me and I couldn't help myself. I don't think anybody ever gets that mad but once. Words came without me knowing what they would be. It was only afterward that I could remember each thing I said and see it all in a clear way.

"Why aren't we buddies? Because you're the dumbest slob I ever saw! Nobody cares anything about you! And just because I felt sorry for you sometimes and tried to act decent don't think I give a damn about a dumb-bunny like you!"

If I talked loud or hit him it wouldn't have been so bad. But my voice was slow and like I was very calm. Sucker's mouth was partway open and he looked as though he'd knocked his funny bone. His face was white and sweat came out on his forehead. He wiped it away with the back of his hand and for a minute his arm stayed raised that way as though he was holding something away from him.

"Don't you know a single thing? Haven't you ever been around at all? Why don't you get a girlfriend instead of me? What kind of sissy do you want to grow up to be anyway?"

I didn't know what was coming next. I couldn't help myself or think.

Sucker didn't move. He had on one of my pajama jackets and his neck stuck out skinny and small. His hair was damp on his forehead.

"Why do you always hang around me? Don't you know when you're not wanted?"

Afterward I could remember the change in Sucker's face. Slowly that blank look went away and he closed his mouth. His eyes got narrow and his fists shut. There had never been such a look on him before. It was like every second he was getting older. There was a hard look to his eyes you don't see usually in a kid. A drop of sweat rolled down his chin and he didn't notice. He just sat there with those eyes on me and he didn't speak and his face was hard and didn't move.

"No you don't know when you're not wanted. You're too dumb. Just like your name—a dumb Sucker." *why name?*

It was like something had busted inside me. I turned off the light and sat down in the chair by the window. My legs were shaking and I was so tired I could have bawled. The room was cold and dark. I sat there for a long time and smoked a squashed cigarette I had saved. Outside the yard was black and quiet. After a while I heard Sucker lie down.

I wasn't mad anymore, only tired. It seemed awful to me that I had talked like that to a kid only twelve. I couldn't take it all in. I told myself I would go over to him and try to make it up. But I just sat there in the cold until a long time had passed. I planned how I could straighten it out in the morning. Then, trying not to squeak the springs, I got back in bed.

Sucker was gone when I woke up the next day. And later when I wanted to apologize as I had planned he looked at me in this new hard way so that I couldn't say a word.

All of that was two or three months ago. Since then Sucker has grown faster than any boy I ever saw. He's almost as tall as I am and his bones have gotten heavier and bigger. He won't wear any of my old clothes anymore and has bought his first pair of long pants—with some leather suspenders to hold them up. Those are just the changes that are easy to see and put into words.

Our room isn't mine at all anymore. He's gotten up this gang of kids and they have a club. When they aren't digging trenches in some vacant lot and fighting they are always in my room. On the door there is some foolishness written in Mercurochrome saying "Woe to the Outsider who Enters" and signed with crossed bones and their secret initials. They have rigged up a radio and every afternoon it blares out music. Once as I was coming in I heard a boy telling something in a low voice about what he saw in the back of his big brother's automobile. I could guess what I didn't hear. *That's what her and my brother do. It's the truth—parked in the car.* For a minute Sucker looked surprised and his face was almost like it used to be. Then he got hard and tough again. "Sure, dumbbell. We know all that." They didn't notice me. Sucker began telling them how in two years he was planning to be a trapper in Alaska.

But most of the time Sucker stays by himself. It is worse when we are alone together in the room. He sprawls across the bed in those long corduroy pants with the suspenders and just stares at me with that hard, half-sneering look. I fiddle around my desk and can't get settled because of those eyes of his. And the thing is I just have to study because I've gotten three bad cards this term already. If I flunk English I can't graduate next year. I don't want to be a bum and I just have to get my mind on it. I don't care a flip for Maybelle or any particular girl anymore and it's only this thing between Sucker and me that is the trouble now. We never speak except when we have to before the family. I don't even want to call him Sucker anymore and unless I forget I call him by his real name, Richard. At night I can't study with him in the room and I have to hang around the drugstore, smoking and doing nothing, with the fellows who loaf there.

More than anything I want to be easy in my mind again. And I miss the way Sucker and I were for a while in a funny, sad way that before this I never would have believed. But everything is so different that there seems to be nothing I can do to get it right. I've sometimes thought if we could have it out in a big fight that would help. But I can't fight him because he's four years younger. And another thing—sometimes this look in his eyes makes me almost believe that if Sucker could he would kill me.

THE POSSIBILITY OF EVIL

Shirley Jackson

Miss Adela Strangeworth stepped daintily along Main Street on her way to the grocery. The sun was shining, the air was fresh and clear after the night's heavy rain, and everything in Miss Strangeworth's little town looked washed and bright. Miss Strangeworth took deep breaths, and thought that there was nothing in the world like a fragrant summer day.

She knew everyone in town, of course; she was fond of telling strangers—tourists who sometimes passed through the town and stopped to admire Miss Strangeworth's roses—that she had never spent more than a day outside this town in all her long life. She was seventy-one, Miss Strangeworth told the tourists, with a pretty little dimple showing by her lip, and she sometimes found herself thinking that the town belonged to her. "My grandfather built the first house on Pleasant Street," she would say, opening her blue eyes wide with the wonder of it. "This house, right here. My family has lived here for better than a hundred years. My grandmother planted these roses, and my mother tended them, just as I do. I've watched my town grow; I can remember when Mr. Lewis, Senior, opened the grocery store, and the year the river flooded out the shanties on the low road, and the excitement when some young folks wanted to move the park over to the space in front of where the new post office is today. They wanted to put up a statue of Ethan Allen"—Miss Strangeworth would frown a little and sound stern—"but it should have been a statue of my grandfather. There wouldn't have been a town here at all if it hadn't been for my grandfather and the lumber mill."

Miss Strangeworth never gave away any of her roses, although the tourists often asked her. The roses belonged on Pleasant Street, and it bothered Miss Strangeworth to think of people wanting to carry them away, to take them into strange towns and down strange streets. When the new minister came, and the ladies were gathering flowers to decorate the church, Miss Strangeworth sent over a great basket of gladioli; when she picked the roses at all, she set them in bowls and vases around the inside of the house her grandfather had built.

Walking down Main Street on a summer morning, Miss Strangeworth had to stop every minute or so to say good morning to someone or to ask after someone's health. When she came into the grocery, half a dozen people turned away from the shelves and the counters to wave at her or call out good morning.

"And good morning to you, too, Mr. Lewis," Miss Strangeworth said at last. The Lewis family had been in the town almost as long as the Strangeworths; but the day young Lewis left high school and went to work in the grocery, Miss Strangeworth had stopped calling him Tommy and started calling him Mr. Lewis, and he had stopped calling her Addie and started calling her Miss Strangeworth. They had been in high school together, and had gone to picnics together, and to high school dances and basketball games; but now Mr. Lewis was behind the counter in the grocery, and Miss Strangeworth was living alone in the Strangeworth house on Pleasant Street.

"Good morning," Mr. Lewis said, and added politely, "lovely day."

"It is a very nice day," Miss Strangeworth said as though she had only just decided that it would do after all. "I would like a chop, please, Mr. Lewis, a small, lean veal chop. Are those strawberries from Arthur Parker's garden? They're early this year."

"He brought them in this morning," Mr. Lewis said.

"I shall have a box," Miss Strangeworth said. Mr. Lewis looked worried, she thought, and for a minute she hesitated, but then she decided that he surely could not be worried over the strawberries. He looked very tired indeed. He was usually so chipper, Miss Strangeworth thought, and almost commented, but it was far too personal a subject to be introduced to Mr. Lewis, the grocer, so she only said, "And a can of cat food and, I think, a tomato."

Silently, Mr. Lewis assembled her order on the counter and waited. Miss Strangeworth looked at him curiously and then said, "It's Tuesday, Mr. Lewis. You forgot to remind me."

"Did I? Sorry."

"Imagine your forgetting that I always buy my tea on Tuesday," Miss Strangeworth said gently. "A quarter pound of tea, please, Mr. Lewis."

"Is that all, Miss Strangeworth?"

"Yes, thank you, Mr. Lewis. Such a lovely day, isn't it?"

"Lovely," Mr. Lewis said.

Miss Strangeworth moved slightly to make room for Mrs. Harper at the counter. "Morning, Adela," Mrs. Harper said, and Miss Strangeworth said, "Good morning, Martha."

"Lovely day," Mrs. Harper said, and Miss Strangeworth said, "Yes, lovely," and Mr. Lewis, under Mrs. Harper's glance, nodded.

"Ran out of sugar for my cake frosting," Mrs. Harper explained. Her hand shook slightly as she opened her pocket-book. Miss Strangeworth wondered, glancing at her quickly, if she had been taking proper care of herself. Martha Harper was not as young as she used to be, Miss Strangeworth thought. She probably could use a good, strong tonic.

"Martha," she said, "you don't look well."

"I'm perfectly all right," Mrs. Harper said shortly. She handed her money to Mr. Lewis, took her change and her sugar, and went out without speaking again. Looking after her, Miss Strangeworth shook her head slightly. Martha definitely did *not* look well.

Carrying her little bag of groceries, Miss Strangeworth came out of the store into the bright sunlight and stopped to smile down on the Crane baby. Don and Helen Crane were really the two most infatuated young parents she had ever known, she thought indulgently, looking at the delicately embroidered baby cap and the lace-edged carriage cover.

"That little girl is going to grow up expecting luxury all her life," she said to Helen Crane.

Helen laughed. "That's the way we want her to feel," she said. "Like a princess."

"A princess can be a lot of trouble sometimes," Miss Strangeworth said dryly. "How old is her highness now?"

"Six months next Tuesday," Helen Crane said, looking down with rapt wonder at her child. "I've been worrying, though, about her. Don't you think she ought to move around more? Try to sit up, for instance?"

"For plain and fancy worrying," Miss Strangeworth said, amused, "give me a new mother every time."

"She just seems—slow," Helen Crane said.

"Nonsense. All babies are different. Some of them develop much more quickly than others."

"That's what my mother says." Helen Crane laughed, looking a little bit ashamed.

"I suppose you've got young Don all upset about the fact that his daughter is already six months old and hasn't yet begun to learn to dance?"

"I haven't mentioned it to him. I suppose she's just so precious that I worry about her all the time."

"Well, apologize to her right now," Miss Strangeworth said. "*She* is probably worrying about why you keep jumping around all the time." Smiling to herself and shaking her old head, she went on down the sunny street, stopping once to ask little Billy Moore why he wasn't out riding in his daddy's shiny new car, and talking for a few minutes outside the library with Miss Chandler, the librarian, about the new novels to be ordered and paid for by the annual library appropriation. Miss Chandler seemed absentminded and very much as though she was thinking about something else. Miss Strangeworth noticed that Miss Chandler had not taken much trouble with her hair that morning, and sighed. Miss Strangeworth hated sloppiness.

Many people seemed disturbed recently, Miss Strangeworth thought. Only yesterday the Stewarts' fifteen-year-old Linda had run crying down her own front walk and all the way to school, not caring who saw her. People around town thought she might have had a fight with the Harris boy, but they showed up together at the soda shop after school as usual, both of them looking grim and bleak. Trouble at home, people concluded, and sighed over the problems of trying to raise kids right these days.

From halfway down the block Miss Strangeworth could catch the heavy scent of her roses, and she moved a little more quickly. The perfume of roses meant home, and home meant the Strangeworth House on Pleasant Street. Miss Strangeworth stopped at her own front gate, as she always did, and looked with deep pleasure at her house, with the red and pink and white roses massed along the narrow lawn, and the rambler going up along the porch; and the neat, the unbelievably trim lines of the house itself, with its slimness and its washed white look. Every window sparkled, every curtain hung stiff and straight, and even the stones of the front walk were swept and clear. People around town wondered how old Miss Strangeworth managed to keep the house looking the way it did, and there was a legend about a tourist once mistaking it for the local museum and going all through the place without finding out about his mistake. But the town was proud of Miss Strangeworth and her roses and her house. They had all grown together. Miss Strangeworth went up her front steps, unlocked her front door with her key, and went into the kitchen to put away her groceries. She debated having a cup of tea and then decided that it was too close to midday dinnertime; she would not have the appetite for her little chop if she had tea now. Instead she went into the light, lovely sitting room, which still glowed from the hands of her mother and her grand-mother, who had covered the chairs with bright chintz and hung the curtains. All the furniture was spare and shining, and the round hooked rugs on the floor had been the work of Miss Strangeworth's grandmother and her mother. Miss Strangeworth had put a bowl of her red roses on the low table before the window, and the room was full of their scent.

Miss Strangeworth went to the narrow desk in the corner, and unlocked it with her key. She never knew when she might feel like writing letters, so she kept her notepaper inside, and the desk locked. Miss Strangeworth's usual stationery was heavy and cream-colored, with "Strangeworth House" engraved across the top, but, when she felt like writing her other letters, Miss Strangeworth used a pad of various-colored paper, bought from the local newspaper shop. It was almost a town joke, that colored paper, layered in pink and green and blue and yellow; everyone in town bought it and used it for odd, informal notes and shopping lists. It was usual to remark, upon receiving a note written on a blue page, that so-and-so would be needing a new pad soon—here she was, down to the blue already. Everyone used the matching envelopes for tucking away recipes, or keeping odd little things in, or even to hold cookies in the school lunchboxes. Mr. Lewis sometimes gave them to the children for carrying home penny candy.

Although Miss Strangeworth's desk held a trimmed quill pen, which had belonged to her grandfather, and a gold-frost fountain pen, which had belonged to her father, Miss Strangeworth always used a dull stub of pencil when she wrote her letters, and she printed them in a childish block print. After thinking for a minute, although she had been phrasing the letter in the back of her mind all the way home, she wrote on a pink sheet: *Didn't you ever see an idiot child before? Some people just shouldn't have children, should they?*

She was pleased with the letter. She was fond of doing things exactly right. When she made a mistake, as she sometimes did, or when the letters were not spaced nicely on the page, she had to take the discarded page to the kitchen stove and burn it at once. Miss Strangeworth never delayed when things had to be done.

After thinking for a minute, she decided that she would like to write another letter, perhaps to go to Mrs. Harper, to follow up the ones she had already mailed. She selected a green sheet this time and wrote quickly: *Have you found out yet what they were all laughing about after you left the bridge club on Thursday? Or is the wife really always the last one to know?*

Miss Strangeworth never concerned herself with facts; her letters all dealt with the more negotiable stuff of suspicion. Mr. Lewis would never have imagined for a minute that his grandson might be lifting petty cash from the store register if he had not had one of Miss Strangeworth's letters. Miss Chandler, the librarian, and Linda Stewart's parents would have gone unsuspectingly ahead with their lives, never aware of possible evil lurking nearby, if Miss Strangeworth had not sent letters to open their eyes. Miss Strangeworth would have been genuinely shocked if there *had* been anything between Linda Stewart and the Harris boy, but, as long as evil existed unchecked in the world, it was Miss Strangeworth's duty to keep her town alert to it. It was far more sensible for Miss Chandler to wonder what Mr. Shelley's first wife had really died of than to take a chance on not knowing. There were so many wicked people in the world and only one Strangeworth left in town. Besides, Miss Strangeworth liked writing her letters.

She addressed an envelope to Don Crane after a moment's thought, wondering curiously if he would show the letter to his wife, and using a pink envelope to match the pink paper. Then she addressed a second envelope, green, to Mrs. Harper. Then an idea came to her and she selected a blue sheet and wrote: *You never know about doctors. Remember they're only human and need money like the rest of us. Suppose the knife slipped accidentally. Would Doctor Burns get his fee and a little extra from that nephew of yours?*

She addressed the blue envelope to old Mrs. Foster, who was having an operation next month. She had thought of writing one more letter, to the head of the school board, asking how a chemistry teacher like Billy Moore's father could afford a new convertible, but all at once she was tired of writing letters. The three she had done would do for one day. She could write more tomorrow; it was not as though they all had to be done at once.

She had been writing her letters—sometimes two or three every day for a week, sometimes no more than one in a month—for the past year. She never got any answers, of course, because she never signed her name. If she had been asked, she would have said that her name, Adela Strangeworth, a name honored in the town for so many years, did not belong on such trash. The town where she lived had to be kept clean and sweet, but people everywhere were lustful and evil and degraded, and needed to be watched; the world was so large, and there was only one Strangeworth left in it. Miss Strangeworth sighed, locked her desk, and put the letters into her big, black leather pocketbook, to be mailed when she took her evening walk.

She broiled her little chop nicely, and had a sliced tomato and good cup of tea ready when she sat down to her midday dinner at the table in her dining room, which could be opened to seat twenty-two, with a second table, if necessary, in the hall. Sitting in the warm sunlight that came through the tall windows of the dining room, seeing her roses massed outside, handling the heavy, old silverware and the fine, translucent china, Miss Strangeworth was pleased; she would not have cared to be doing anything else. People must live graciously, after all, she thought, and sipped her tea. Afterward, when her plate and cup and saucer were washed and dried and put back onto the shelves where they belonged, and her silverware was back in the mahogany silver chest, Miss Strangeworth went up the graceful staircase and into her bedroom, which was the front room overlooking the roses, and had been her mother's and her grandmother's. Their Crown Derby dresser set and furs had been kept here, their fans and silver-backed brushes and their own bowls of roses; Miss Strangeworth kept a bowl of white roses on the bed table.

She drew the shades, took the rose satin spread from the bed, slipped out of her dress and her shoes, and lay down tiredly. She knew that no doorbell or phone would ring; no one in town would dare to disturb Miss Strangeworth during her afternoon nap. She slept, deep in the rich smell of roses.

After her nap she worked in her garden for a little while, sparing herself because of the heat; then she went in to her supper. She ate asparagus from her own garden, with sweet-butter sauce, and a soft-boiled egg, and, while she had her supper, she listened to a late-evening news broadcast and then to a program of classical music on her small radio. After her dishes were done and her kitchen set in order, she took up her hat—Miss Strangeworth's hats were proverbial in the town; people believed that she had inherited them from her mother and her grandmother—and, locking the front door of her house behind her, set off on her evening walk, pocketbook under her arm. She nodded to Linda Stewart's father, who was washing his car in the pleasantly cool evening. She thought that he looked troubled.

There was only one place in town where she could mail her letters, and that was the new post office, shiny with red brick and silver letters. Although Miss Strangeworth had never given the matter any particular thought, she had always made a point of mailing her letters very secretly; it would, of course, not have been wise to let anyone see her mail them. Consequently, she timed her walk so she could reach the post office just as darkness was starting to dim the outlines of the trees and the shapes of people's faces, although no one could ever mistake Miss Strangeworth, with her dainty walk and her rustling skirts.

There was always a group of young people around the post office, the very youngest roller-skating upon its driveway, which went all the way around the building and was the only smooth road in town; and the slightly older ones already knowing how to gather in small groups and chatter and laugh and make great, excited plans for going across the street to the soda shop in a minute or two. Miss Strangeworth had never had any self-consciousness before the children. She did not feel that any of them were staring at her unduly or longing to laugh at her; it would have been most reprehensible for their parents to permit their children to mock Miss Strangeworth of Pleasant Street. Most of the children stood back respectfully as Miss Strangeworth passed, silenced briefly in her presence, and some of the older children greeted her, saying soberly, "Hello, Miss Strangeworth."

Miss Strangeworth smiled at them and quickly went on. It had been a long time since she had known the name of every child in town. The mail slot was in the door of the post office. The children stood away as Miss Strangeworth approached it, seemingly surprised that anyone should want to use the post office after it had been officially closed up for the night and turned over to the children. Miss Strangeworth stood by the door, opening her black pocketbook to take out the letters, and heard a voice which she knew at once to be Linda Stewart's. Poor little Linda was crying again, and Miss Strangeworth listened carefully. This was, after all, her town, and these were her people; if one of them was in trouble, she ought to know about it.

"I can't tell you, Dave," Linda was saying—so she *was* talking to the Harris boy, as Miss Strangeworth had supposed—"I just *can't*. It's just *nasty*."

"But why won't your father let me come around anymore? What on earth did I do?"

"I can't tell you. I just wouldn't tell you for *any*thing. You've got to have a dirty dirty mind for things like that."

"But something's happened. You've been crying and crying, and your father is all upset. Why can't *I* know about it, too? Aren't I like one of the family?"

"Not anymore, Dave, not anymore. You're not to come near our house again; my father said so. He said he'd horsewhip you. That's all I can tell you: You're not to come near our house anymore."

"But I didn't *do* anything."

"Just the same, my father said . . ."

Miss Strangeworth sighed and turned away. There was so much evil in people. Even in a charming little town like this one, there was still so much evil in people.

She slipped her letters into the slot, and two of them fell inside. The third caught on the edge and fell outside, onto the ground at Miss Strangeworth's feet. She did not notice it because she was wondering whether a letter to the Harris boy's father might not be of some service in wiping out this potential badness. Wearily Miss Strangeworth turned to go home to her quiet bed in her lovely house, and never heard the Harris boy calling to her to say that she had dropped something.

"Old lady Strangeworth's getting deaf," he said, looking after her and holding in his hand the letter he had picked up.

"Well, who cares?" Linda said. "Who cares anymore, anyway?"

"It's for Don Crane," the Harris boy said, "this letter. She dropped a letter addressed to Don Crane. Might as well take it on over. We pass his house anyway." He laughed. "Maybe it's got a check or something in it and he'd be just as glad to get it tonight instead of tomorrow."

"Catch old lady Strangeworth sending anybody a check," Linda said. "Throw it in the post office. Why do anyone a favor?" She sniffed. "Doesn't seem to me anybody around here cares about us," she said. "Why should we care about them?"

"I'll take it over, anyway," the Harris boy said. "Maybe it's good news for them. Maybe they need something happy tonight, too. Like us."

Sadly, holding hands, they wandered off down the dark street, the Harris boy carrying Miss Strangeworth's pink envelope in his hand.

Miss Strangeworth awakened the next morning with a feeling of intense happiness and, for a minute, wondered why, and then remembered that this morning three people would open her letters. Harsh, perhaps, at first, but wickedness was never easily banished, and a clean heart was a scoured heart. She washed her soft, old face and brushed her teeth, still sound in spite of her seventy-one years, and dressed herself carefully in her sweet, soft clothes and buttoned shoes. Then, going downstairs, reflecting that perhaps a little waffle would be agreeable for breakfast in the sunny dining room, she found the mail on the hall floor, and bent to pick it up. A bill, the morning paper, a letter in a green envelope that looked oddly familiar. Miss Strangeworth stood perfectly still for a minute, looking down at the green envelope with the penciled printing, and thought:

It looks like one of my letters. Was one of my letters sent back? No, because no one would know where to send it. How did this get here?

Miss Strangeworth was a Strangeworth of Pleasant Street. Her hand did not shake as she opened the envelope and unfolded the sheet of green paper inside. She began to cry silently for the wickedness of the world when she read the words: *Look out at what used to be your roses.*

SUPERSTITIONS

Mary La Chapelle

Frances slept in her clothes. This was a recent practice she had adopted from Jimmy after finding him one morning under his covers outfitted in his miniature army costume. As he popped out of his covers and swung his weedy legs over the bed, his sister was further puzzled to see his feet still shod in his little army boots.

"Jimmy, they're muddy."

He had looked at his dangling feet and reached down to flick a piece of dirt encrusted in the soles of his boots.

"Why did you wear play clothes to bed?"

"I always do." He hopped off his bed and began tapping his boot against the bedstead, causing the mud to flake off in a pile on the floor.

"Well, I know you didn't always. Why do you want to?"

"Simple, Franny, that way I'm ready to play as soon as I wake up."

Now for the last three days, Frances had slept in her red Buster Brown shirt and her light-blue cutoffs. As she meandered into wakefulness, she found a specific comfort in fingering the familiar clothing.

It was an early June morning, a week into the summer vacation. Frances held on to her sleep even as the sun came into her bedroom and lay across her forehead like a warm rag. But when the light became so bright that she needed to cover her eyes with her arm, she woke up and rolled onto one elbow so she could rest her chin on the window ledge by her bed. She blinked her eyes. From two stories up the grass looked wavy like water.

Frances turned from the window and looked around the squareness of her room. Reassured that she had gone nowhere else in the night, she slipped out of her tight covers from the top. This was another time-saving trick Jimmy had taught her. He theorized that little kids who got in from the top and out from the top never had to make their beds. "Just punch the pillow and that is that."

She stood for a moment by the bed and looked out at the day-to-be. In the sky two swallows spiraled erratically downward. They looked more to be falling than flying. Away from the window she turned to face the half-open door.

She closed her eyes and touched her fingers to the wall just above her bedpost, then walked like this, eyes closed, her one hand guiding her along the wall out of her room and down the hall. She was apprehensive as she brushed on toward the attic, because if she were to find it had been left open, it would be a bad sign that she couldn't change. Her hand hesitated at the doorway molding as a draft wafted over the little hairs on her wrist. The door was open. She passed her hand over empty space, making believe there was a door there. This didn't help, and the panic she had dreaded surged up from her stomach, making her run blindly down the hall until she was at the opening of the stairway. She bent over to feel where the first step began and sat down on the landing. Her eyes were still closed, she pressed them against her knees, and the pressure created white lights under her eyelids.

This ritual of the blind walk through the upstairs hall was one Frances had adopted herself. She had not taught it to Jimmy because it made no sense. Just as it made no sense to be afraid of an open attic. It was something she had begun, and now she was compelled to continue.

Frances sat at the top of the stairs with her eyes pressed against her knees. Something bad was going to happen, and there was nothing she could do about it. She was trying not to think about the attic, and she wished she had never made up the rule. She muttered aloud, "I just made it up. It's silly, so nothing can happen."

Frances found no one in the kitchen, but she heard sounds indicating that the others were out of bed. Her father was at work. Her mother was in the sewing room in the basement. She could hear the steady whirr of the machine, and then it stopped, shortly to be replaced by the sound of scissors snipping. The racket of cartoons was coming from the TV room along with Jimmy's shrill giggles. Frances chose a firm banana from the bunch on the counter and went to join her brother.

Frances once heard her mother confide to Mrs. Benson that Jimmy was hyperactive. Her grandmother called him high-strung. Frances liked to watch his green eyes when they danced on the wake of one of his ideas. His freckles, too, they danced. Or it seemed to Frances, at least, that they moved about on his face, and as long as she needed to blink she would never be sure.

Jimmy's black hair was controlled by some strange static that caused it to stand up in little tufts, always, as if he had just taken off a wool stocking cap. His father would wet it and comb it, saying, "Kiddo, we are going to train your hair to stay put." But half an hour later Jimmy's hair would be sticking up all over again.

Frances believed that Jimmy had more God-given life than she had. It was the bravery that made the difference. He had more life to risk than she had, and she stayed close to him for need of the bravery.

Of the two, Frances thought she was the stronger. She was tall with the dark skin of her Indian grandmother. Jimmy was fair, his skin translucent, the veins lying close to the surface. He was slight and smaller than he should be for his age. Sometimes she would use this against him and say, "I'm ten and you're a puny eight-year-old." But that was only when she felt the least brave in the face of him. The times she did feel truly stronger, she said nothing. Sometimes as they sat arm against arm on the sofa, and he looked ahead distracted by the TV, she would trace the veins in his fine hand with her finger, and that quiet tenderness would come over her. She would move closer to him and cover his whole arm with her own, laying her brown hand over his so each of her fingers covered one of his, and nothing was left exposed.

His energy overflowed the confines of his body sometimes, like popcorn popping out of a pot too small. On the day that the Bensons' cat had kittens, Jimmy had come running up the back-porch steps where Frances and her mother sat trimming rhubarb. He stopped, breathless, on the top step, making little hops and shaking in the shoulders. He opened his mouth but could only stutter, "The, the ca . . . c."

Their mother said, "Now, Jimmy, calm down."

He made a short whistling sound through his skinny nose and tried again. "Th . . . th . . . th . . ."

"Jimmy," their mother said crossly. "Stop. Think about what you are trying to say."

Then he did stop, stopped hopping; he stopped shaking, while his eyes ceased to dance and rolled back as though to see what he was trying to say. He fell then, crumpled down like a kite that lost its wind. His tremors began before their mother reached him, and she hesitated as though she was afraid to touch him. Frances looked down from the top step at her brother's closed eyes. She could see violent movement beneath the faint blue skin of his eyelids. In a moment he was calm. When he opened his eyes, they were dull, duller than the time he had been sleeping and Frances had peeled his eyes open to see what was in there.

Jimmy took two different pills now to control his seizures. Their mother kept the bottles stored in a square Tupperware container up in the kitchen cupboard next to the Kool-Aid packages and the Green Stamps. Twice Frances had climbed on the counter to look at the pills. She took them out of their bottles to touch them, and the second time she almost took one, but she decided against it and put them back.

Jimmy didn't have any more big seizures. But once in a while he had a little one, and he would nod over his dinner plate. He'd snap his head up just in time and then just go on as though nothing had happened. Sometimes his eyes would close while he was watching television, and if Frances saw him, she would wonder how much he had missed. Jimmy himself seemed the least concerned about it.

Their mother worried, and she let Frances know that it was the daughter's job to worry when the mother was not around. So Frances put this worry in the back of her head with all her other worries. Though, after a while, she did not think specifically about his seizures, the fear she felt that first day she had seen him lose himself hovered in her dreams—dreams of reaching for him before he fell into some blackness and out of her dream. Her nightmares were forgotten in the daytime, but she began to feel more irritated with him, concerned about his uncontrollable ways. And he didn't like it when she cared so much, called her "Bossy" and "Miss Big Business Beeswax."

Frances leaned against the TV room doorway. She peeled her banana and watched her brother's back. He sat forward in the rocker, his boots just touching the floor. A large bowl of cereal was perched on his knees. She couldn't see his face, but she knew what he looked like. His eyes were opened wide, absorbed, connected to the action on the television, and his mouth was the part of him eating cereal, eating vigorously. Sometimes he would forget, laugh at the cartoon, and milk would dribble out of the corner of his mouth.

Frances waited for Jimmy to finish with his cereal. Then she placed her banana skin in the wastebasket by the door, crouched over, and crept up behind his rocker. Gently, she took hold of the top of his chair and placed each of her bare feet over the rockers. She leaned back, causing her little brother to slide back in the chair and look up at her. "Gimme a ride, Jimmy."

"Well, Jell-O, Franny. It's about time."

She moved about the room, then stopped to stand a bit in front of the television so he would pay attention to her.

"Is it going to be a TV day?" she challenged.

"No way, Ray!" Jimmy twisted around in his chair so that his head was soon hanging where his feet had been and his skinny feet were poked through the back rungs of the chair. His hands, still holding the cereal bowl, dangled close to the floor. Then he rocked himself just enough to set the bowl down.

"What are we going to do?" She was getting impatient.

"War games," he said.

"What kind?"

"We're going to take an important bridge."

"Jimmy, there is only one bridge, and we already took it."

"Not this one, we didn't."

"Where is it?"

Jimmy gave an upside-down smile, grunted; his face was red with little white patches where the veins stood out on his forehead.

"Is it over the river? Jimmy! Stop doing that! You're all purple. Answer me, is it over the river?" She grabbed his arms, pulling him out of the chair onto the floor. He breathed heavily and giggled a bit as his face faded to a more agreeable shade. Frances plopped herself into the rocker and began rocking, giving his bony butt a light kick every time she rocked forward. "For the last time, is it over the river?"

"Don't worry. I'll show you," he said, a smug expression on his face.

"So I suppose that means you are going to be the leader?"

"Yeah," he said, grabbing her ankles and pretending to bite them.

"Jimmy, you were the leader yesterday."

"No, I wasn't. Scotty Tanner was."

"Well, let's both be leaders," she said.

"We can't both be. I'll be the leader before the bridge, and you be the leader after the bridge."

"We need more men," she said, as she fantasized being the leader of a larger group.

"Nope. This is a secret maneuver. We can't have everybody in the neighborhood knowing about it."

"Oh, big deal."

"Hey! You're supposed to obey me now."

"Okay, okay, so let's go," she surrendered, giving him one last kick from the rocker.

This last kick spurred Jimmy, and he blasted up from the floor in one swift movement. He stood in front of Frances, his legs spread with his little knees hyperextended in back. She knew immediately, by looking at him, that he was already playing. He was playing soldier.

He pulled his thumbs through the empty belt loops of his fatigue pants and pressed his other four knuckles into his hips. As he stared her down, Frances resisted. Her eyes started to laugh at him. She wanted to protest and call him silly. But the largest part of her wanted to be drawn into his fantasy, and this turned her expression to expectation. She waited.

Jimmy leaned her chair back. "All right then, we're going to take an important bridge today. It's over the river, like you thought, but it's not a common bridge. I think, mostly, that people don't know about it. So once we take it, it'll be our bridge, and the territory on the other side'll be our territory. Now, I'll get the supplies, and you tell the home office."

Frances went down the basement stairs to her mother's sewing room. Her mother, the home officer, surveyed Frances from across her sewing table and then bowed to her sewing again.

"Frances, when are you going to change your clothes?"

"I don't know."

"Well, I hope you'll know soon."

Her mother concentrated on changing the needle in her machine.

"Mom?"

"Mm, hmm?"

"Jimmy and I are going out to play."

"Where is out?"

"Oh, you know."

"I know that you are to stay away from the banks. Stay up on the trails. Before you go, take this up to Jimmy." She handed Frances an old leather belt of their father's, trimmed down with extra holes poked into it. "Tell him to wear it. I have had enough of droopy drawers and everybody in the neighborhood seeing where his legs begin." Her mother looked over her sewing glasses to make the point, then resumed her work.

Frances held the belt in her hand. But instead of moving away, back to Jimmy, she waited as though her mother might have something more to give her. She leaned against the sewing table.

"Frances, don't jiggle the table. How can I sew a straight line?"

"Mom?"

"Hmm?" Her mother now had pins between her lips.

"Sister Margaret Therase said that God knows all our thoughts the very second that we think them."

"Mm, hmm." Her mother bent her head close to the sewing machine needle and pushed a black thread through the tiny hole.

"Sometimes I have bad thoughts. I don't mean to think them, but, you know, they just come to me, and then, I suppose, he knows. I try to take it back . . ."

"Take what back?" her mother mumbled, with the pins still between her lips.

"The bad thoughts." Frances moved up to her mother and plucked the three pins altogether out of her mouth. "Now, talk to me."

"Well, Frances, if it's important, why don't you start from the beginning and try to make yourself a little more clear?"

Frances sighed, closed one eye, looked at her mother. "Sometimes I have bad thoughts." She announced this sentence, each word stated loudly and with long pauses in between, as though her mother might be hard of hearing or slow-witted. "I don't think them on purpose, and I wish that God would just forget about them so that I won't be in trouble."

"Well, just tell God you're sorry. Go to Saturday confession." Her mother smiled at Frances.

"Nooo," Frances bleated. "Not those kinds of bad thoughts, not sinful or mean ones."

"Are you talking about impure thoughts?"

"Ahh!"

"Well, honey, you're not being very clear then. Can't you give me an example?"

Frances cleared her throat. "Okay, we'll be riding in the car. We're passing underneath the stoplight, and just then the stoplight changes to yellow. Well, the first time that happened to us, I got the bad thought."

"What bad thought?"

"Just that it is bad luck to be under the light when you can't see it change to yellow, and if I ever do that again, something bad will happen."

"Like what will happen, Frances? Would we be in a car accident then?"

Frances pictured in her mind what a car accident might be like. She looked up at the ceiling to see what else the bad thing might be.

"I don't know, Mom. Bad is bad. I just get scared. I think the thought about something not going the right way, and then the next thing I think is, Oh, no, now God knows it, and he is going to make it a rule."

"A rule?"

"Yes, a rule! A rule!" Frances pulled at the bottom of her red knit shirt with her hands and stretched it almost to the bottom of her shorts as she strained to be clear. "I make the rule up first, which isn't so bad, but if God hears it, and you know he always does, he's the one that can make the bad thing happen. Do you see?"

"No."

Frances leaned her elbows on the sewing table and cradled her forehead in her hands. She thought about lying in her bed at night and how the hall light shone in through her door. She couldn't sleep with the light shining in her eyes, but she was afraid to sleep in the dark, too. She remembered when she had first found the solution to the problem. She had gotten up and moved the door to the position of being exactly half open and half closed. But as soon as she had done that, a new rule had entered her consciousness. Exactly in the middle, that was what the rule had been after that. From then on she had to remember to keep the door exactly in the middle when she went to bed, or somehow it would be bad luck.

Frances felt her mother touch her elbow, and she heard her say, "Tell me."

She looked up, still holding her chin in her hand and said, "Like for instance, the bedroom door has to be half open. That's not a bad one though, not as bad as the stoplight one anyway. I suppose the bigger the bad luck, the worse the bad thing that is going to happen. I think little ones hardly count, but I do them just the same to be safe."

"Give me an example of a little one."

"Eating M&M's."

"What about M&M's, for heaven sakes?" her mother asked.

"I have to eat them in order. I lay them all out in rows by color. I eat the M&M's from the longer rows until all the rows are the same length as the shortest row." Frances was finding this a difficult process to explain. "In other words, until there is the same number of each color left. Then I eat one from the red row, one from yellow, one from the brown, never changing the order, until they're all gone."

"Frances, look at me. Those rules you are worried about are just superstitions, like walking under ladders and breaking mirrors. Lord knows why you have to make up your own. Maybe we all do at one time or other."

Frances looked at her mother, and her mother looked back kindly through her sewing glasses. Frances looked down again at Jimmy's belt and felt the sadness of being misunderstood. "Mom?"

"What, dear?" she said as she leaned toward the sewing machine and pushed the blue fabric under the needle.

"I had a bad superstition this morning, and I just can't help feeling that God is going to take me up on it."

"But God is good," her mother said. "Don't worry about that."

Frances heard Jimmy rattling the basement stair railing, sending her signals that he was waiting for her to join him. Their mother heard him too. She raised her head from her work and shouted above to the first floor. "Jimmy! There is no point in sneaking around. I know about your little expedition to the river, and all I can say—and I've told Frances, too—is that you are to stay on the upper trails."

Jimmy made high, whining noises like the sounds of radio frequency and shouted back down the basement, "I can't read you—am experiencing interference."

"Well, you better read me, fella," she called back.

They heard Jimmy shout, "AWOL!"

"When you go up there, tell your brother no more shouting."

Frances didn't answer her. Still leaning on the table, she spent a lot of time sticking each of the pins that she still held into her mother's pincushion.

Her mother glanced up. "You're such a moody bird, Frances." Frances rolled her eyes and walked away from the sewing table with a sort of underhanded wave. It was a wave to half-say goodbye and to half-say get lost. She stomped up the stairs to let her mother know that she was leaving and to let her brother know that she was coming.

Jimmy was sitting on the top step. His legs on the second step were jiggling up and down in his little army boots. Jimmy's body commotion had caused several of the supply items to fall from his lap. Frances said, "Jeez, Jimmy," as she alternately climbed the last few steps and picked up the fallen objects. She picked up one of her high-top tennis shoes. Jimmy had painted it completely black with a Magic Marker so the pair would match his army boots. There was also a little tin compass, which always said North unless someone shook it—then it said Northwest. The last thing was a long, narrow strip of paper that had a representation of the Mississippi River running down it. Jimmy had cut this out of a larger map of the United States in their family atlas. Frances wished that he would throw it away. It was hardly an aid to their minute explorations of the river.

While Frances put her shoes on, Jimmy stood in the back hallway, listing aloud the supplies as he stuck them in his baggy pockets. "Peanut butter and grahams, compass, map, twine, penlight, jackknife, a banana for me, and here is a banana for you."

Frances stood up, took the banana that Jimmy was handing her, and stuck it in the elastic of her shorts. "Here, Mom wants you to wear this," she said, while threading Jimmy's new belt through his belt loops.

"Nice." He hummed a note of pleasure, stuck his banana through his belt and patted it as though it was a pistol. "Ready, Eddy?" Jimmy asked Frances.

"You bet, pet." Frances stretched her brown arms over his little shoulders and walked him backward out of the back screen door.

On the stoop they both leaned down to pick up their walking sticks. Jimmy had smoothed them out by rubbing them against the concrete driveway. That was in the spring, and now the two sticks had become a part of their routine. Frances was fond of her stick; she liked its sanded softness. She thought, as she gripped the stick and walked with Jimmy out of the backyard, that the stick made being outside easier. It was not a superstition. Her stick was useful. She could test the depth of puddles before walking through them, turn night crawlers over on the sidewalk without getting the slime on her fingers. She could knock crab apples out of the trees, and she could knock any wise guy in the neighborhood if need be.

Jimmy cherished his stick as an object of fantasy. Frances couldn't keep up with its many identities: a sword, a staff, a laser gun. When Jimmy wanted to pretend sword fighting with her, she would resist, saying, "I don't want to break my stick."

They walked a short distance along the back fences of the neighboring yards and turned from the alley onto the sidewalk. They headed for the river, which was five straight blocks away. The sun was warm and persistent with promises to shine over everything by noon. Frances stood flat-footed for a moment, pulling up the heat of the sidewalk through her tennis shoes.

Outside, Jimmy forgot himself completely. Frances forgot herself occasionally. She was aware of certain precautions, like not looking into the sun too long.

"Crack, Jimmy, don't step on the crack!"

"Crack smack."

"You'll break somebody's back!"

"Not mine."

"Somebody's. Just play the game. Play it for me."

"Okay, crack shmack, crack smack," and he jumped on every crack he could see.

"Jimmy!" She grabbed him around the waist tightly with her chin between his shoulder blades. He giggled, then stopped. Frances breathed warm breaths through the shirt on his back. He made low growling sounds like a captured lion.

Frances held Jimmy in a grip that said, You can't get away. She might have held him forever, but he slumped down, making himself deadweight in her arms. He hummed a teasing little tune between his teeth. And while Frances became nervous about his tune, he slumped down just far enough to dangle his hands close to the inside of her knees. Then, when he had gained his position, he tickled her relentlessly there. They both fell to the grass boulevard next to the sidewalk and laughed until they ached. When they rolled away from each other onto their backs, she found banana smashed on the front of her shorts and shirt.

Frances scraped the mash disgustedly off of her clothes and wiped it onto the grass with her fingers. She saw that Jimmy's banana had also exploded at the top, and she caught him by the arm, as he rolled toward her, to save him from the mess.

"Watch out for the banana."

"Eyugh!" Jimmy feigned repulsion, and then, making his eyes wicked, he took the banana in his hands like a cake decorator and squeezed it onto her bare leg.

"God! You're such a goon. Why do I ever think we can be friends?"

Flat on her back, Frances draped her arm across her brow and looked at the sky. The sun was indeed getting higher, and she moved her arm over her eyes to block its glare. The weight of her arm against her eyelids brought the white lights back again, and she remembered the morning's early omen. "Let's go to the Connor wading pool instead," she said, without looking at him.

"No, I'm going to the bridge."

The day wasn't going her way, though she wasn't sure what her way would be. She was just feeling hot and listless.

"I don't want to go." She yanked the grass by her sides and looked at the sky again. Jimmy stood up to leave. There was no argument. She turned on her side a little to watch him, and as he walked away, he turned his black, bristly head ever so slightly and spoke the word that controlled her.

"Chicken."

She lay there with her face in the grass, saw a small black ant crawling with quivering effort up one of the narrow blades. After waiting for what she perceived as a stubborn enough amount of time, she stood up and followed him.

On the sidewalk ahead she could barely make out the figure of Jimmy with his stick by his side. She wasn't worried about catching up with him eventually. At least she knew she would along the riverbank somewhere. She began to smell the river in the warm air as she walked forward. Her gradual anticipation of its sun-glinted surface took the place, step by step, of her former negative disposition. She forgot temporarily about the cracks in the sidewalk.

The river was the biggest thing Frances knew about. It frustrated her that Jimmy didn't understand how big it was. To him, it was a skinny thing cut out of the atlas, and she believed that he didn't think it had much to do with the rest of the country now that he had cut it out of there and kept it folded up in his pocket. They had argued about its size, but Jimmy still insisted that Lake Minnetonka was much bigger.

Once they crossed University Avenue, it was only a block to the river. As she waited there for traffic to pass, she studied a billboard posted on a building across the street. It was a picture of three men with various kinds of headgear and uniforms. The caption in the lower right-hand corner simply said, "Join the Army." She thought of Jimmy, whom she had lost sight of a few blocks back. Now she wasn't so sure she would catch up with him before he took off on his mission. What if she lost him? She pulled her stick up under her arm and broke into a run. She ran between cars to the other side of the street. Her legs were strong, and the spring in her calves excited the rest of her body.

When Frances came finally to the bluff, she felt small. The cityscape loomed at her from the other side of the river. In the foreground, along the opposite bank, there were many structures of industry—cranes, cables, electrical towers, black skeletal constructions that were menacing to Frances, even in the daytime.

Frances peered over the bluff and called down to the trails, but her voice was lost in the river, and Jimmy didn't answer. She suspected he'd taken the lower trails closest to the water where a bridge might be found. She descended steep stone steps and then made her way along the path beside the water. Next she chose a path that took her higher up to the middle ground. There she stopped and looked around her.

The bluffs overhead were built up with limestone walls to support the mill buildings on top. The numerous tunnels that pierced the upper walls, once used for drainage, were cracked and dry. A pair of pigeons fluttered out of one of these cavelike

openings, and their racket startled her. She bent her head back
to watch them. The sun behind them glared in her eyes so that
her vision was shattered a moment with white specks. "Jimmy!"
Where was he? She called again, her voice bouncing off the
wall. She thought she heard something, but then it was lost.
Then she was sure she had heard it. A small faint "Hey!" He
was above somewhere, but she couldn't see him. She looked
higher up to the sound and spotted him. Her stomach jumped
when she saw how high he was.

He was balanced against the sky on an old iron girder that
stretched out from the mouth of one of the upper caves to the
protruding rock of another bluff. The girder looked so narrow
that Jimmy appeared to be suspended in air. As she looked at
him, the sun blinded her again, and she couldn't bear it.

There wasn't time to take the trail back to the steps, so she
began to climb the rocks at the foot of the bluff. Her ears were
full of her own breathing, and with each breath she would call
out to herself, "That's not a bridge. That's not a bridge. That's
not a bridge." The closer she came to Jimmy's position, the
more panicky she became, and her refrain turned to, "This
is the bad thing. This is the bad thing." But then she caught
herself and changed it to, "No, it's not. No, I won't let it be.
No, I won't let you do it." She was losing her breath when she
finally reached the upper trail. She ran along the upper trail
until she was below the cave.

Jimmy was still teetering on the girder. His back was to
her, and he was bowed slightly, looking down. She didn't call
to him, afraid to startle him. Now she could see how he'd got
there. He'd climbed down instead of up. There was even a
sort of rock trail coming down from the high ground. A ledge
jutted out from the wall in front of the archway of the cave. It
was from this ledge that the girder was suspended.

It was necessary for Frances to climb the wall from below. It wasn't far up now, but it took time for her to search out the proper footholds. Normally, she would have been frightened of such a climb, but today she was frightened for Jimmy. Today she was sure the bad luck was his. Once, her footing slipped on a rock, but her hand grips were strong enough to hold her.

When she climbed over the ledge, Jimmy was watching her from his perch.

"Hey, good going, Franny. I've been waiting for you."

Frances gave him no reaction. She could see how rusty and decayed the girder was and understood how easily it could fall apart. She looked only briefly at the drop Jimmy was hanging over. He was above a small ravine full of rocks and other rusted beams that had fallen like this one would.

Frances wanted to sound calm when she first spoke. She wanted not to be afraid. She thought perhaps she could change the bad luck if she wasn't afraid.

Her stick still hung from her belt loops. She knew what she should do. "Jimmy, I want you to come back here." She leaned out over the ravine. "I want you to hold on to this stick and cross back over here."

"No way, Ray. The idea is to cross this bridge."

Frances couldn't keep her voice level. "Jimmy, please."

He looked back at her, with challenge in his face. "And I say, Franny!" He began to bounce on the girder singing, "Franny, Franny, Franny." He was teasing. Across the short expanse she could see the dance in his eyes. Then there was a change. A curtain began to close over the dance, and she knew it was starting to happen. Jimmy knew what was happening too. A shred of a second before his eyes went blank, she could see the terrible fear, the kind that she had never, never seen on his face before.

She was on the girder before he began to stumble. When he did begin to lose his balance, she shouted with a deep voice, a voice not her own, "Hold on to the bridge."

Perhaps her words made him respond, or perhaps his own little body responded independently in that dawning moment before the seizure—that time between control and uncontrol. Something forced him to his knees, kept him from toppling over.

Frances straddled the girder and grabbed his belt. She stuck her stick through the belt and used it for a handle as she inched her way backward on the beam. She waited a little as he shuddered, and when he began to come to, she pulled him off the girder onto the ledge.

Groggy, but conscious now, Jimmy cried like a wounded soldier, all anguish and failure in something he didn't understand. He cried like it was a new thing to cry.

She laid her body across his and was quiet.

Jimmy said in small chokes, "I wet it, Franny, I wet my uniform." She felt the dampness too, but she kept herself from crying because she was the older one. She was the one who knew how these things could happen.

She nestled her face next to his and said, "That's okay, Jimmy, we can change it when we get home."

GRYPHON

Charles Baxter

On Wednesday afternoon, between the geography lesson on ancient Egypt's hand-operated irrigation system and an art project that involved drawing a model city next to a mountain, our fourth-grade teacher, Mr. Hibler, developed a cough. This cough began with a series of muffled throat-clearings and progressed to propulsive noises contained within Mr. Hibler's closed mouth. "Listen to him," Carol Peterson whispered to me. "He's gonna blow up." Mr. Hibler's laughter—dazed and infrequent—sounded a bit like his cough, but as we worked on our model cities we would look up, thinking he was enjoying a joke, and see Mr. Hibler's face turning red, his cheeks puffed out. This was not laughter. Twice he bent over, and his loose tie, like a plumb line, hung down straight from his neck as he exploded himself into a Kleenex. He would excuse himself, then go on coughing. "I'll bet you a dime," Carol Peterson whispered, "we get a substitute tomorrow."

Carol sat at the desk in front of mine and was a bad person— when she thought no one was looking she would blow her nose on notebook paper, then crumple it up and throw it into the wastebasket—but at times of crisis she spoke the truth. I knew I'd lose the dime.

"No deal," I said.

When Mr. Hibler stood us in formation at the door just prior to the final bell, he was almost incapable of speech. "I'm sorry, boys and girls," he said. "I seem to be coming down with something."

"I hope you feel better tomorrow, Mr. Hibler," Bobby Kryzanowicz, the faultless brownnoser, said, and I heard Carol Peterson's evil giggle. Then Mr. Hibler opened the door and we walked out to the buses, a clique of us starting noisily to hawk and raugh as soon as we thought we were a few feet beyond Mr. Hibler's earshot.

Since Five Oaks was a rural community, and in Michigan, the supply of substitute teachers was limited to the town's unemployed community college graduates, a pool of about four mothers. These ladies fluttered, provided easeful class days, and nervously covered material we had mastered weeks earlier. Therefore it was a surprise when a woman we had never seen came into class the next day, carrying a purple purse, a checkerboard lunchbox, and a few books. She put the books on one side of Mr. Hibler's desk and the lunchbox on the other, next to the Voice of Music phonograph. Three of us in the back of the room were playing with Heever, the chameleon that lived in a terrarium and on one of the plastic drapes, when she walked in.

She clapped her hands at us. "Little boys," she said, "why are you bent over together like that?" She didn't wait for us to answer. "Are you tormenting an animal? Put it back. Please sit down at your desks. I want no cabals this time of the day." We just stared at her. "Boys," she repeated, "I asked you to sit down."

I put the chameleon in his terrarium and felt my way to my desk, never taking my eyes off the woman. With white and green chalk, she had started to draw a tree on the left side of the blackboard. She didn't look usual. Furthermore, her tree was outsized, disproportionate, for some reason.

"This room needs a tree," she said, with one line drawing the suggestion of a leaf. "A large, leafy, shady, deciduous . . . oak."

Her fine, light hair had been done up in what I would learn years later was called a chignon, and she wore gold-rimmed glasses whose lenses seemed to have the faintest blue tint. Harold Knardahl, who sat across from me, whispered, "Mars," and I nodded slowly, savoring the imminent weirdness of the day. The substitute drew another branch with an extravagant arm gesture, then turned around and said, "Good morning. I don't believe I said good morning to all of you yet."

Facing us, she was no special age—an adult is an adult—but her face had two prominent lines, descending vertically from the sides of her mouth to her chin. I knew where I had seen those lines before: *Pinocchio.* They were marionette lines. "You may stare at me," she said to us, as a few more kids from the last bus came into the room, their eyes fixed on her, "for a few more seconds, until the bell rings. Then I will permit no more staring. Looking I will permit. Staring, no. It is impolite to stare, and a sign of bad breeding. You cannot make a social effort while staring."

Harold Knardahl did not glance at me, or nudge, but I heard him whisper "Mars" again, trying to get more mileage out of his single joke with the kids who had just come in.

When everyone was seated, the substitute teacher finished her tree, put down her chalk fastidiously on the phonograph, brushed her hands, and faced us. "Good morning," she said. "I am Miss Ferenczi, your teacher for the day. I am fairly new to your community, and I don't believe any of you know me. I will therefore start by telling you a story about myself."

While we settled back, she launched into her tale. She said her grandfather had been a Hungarian prince; her mother had been born in some place called Flanders, had been a pianist, and had played concerts for people Miss Ferenczi referred to as "crowned heads." She gave us a knowing look. "Grieg," she said, "the Norwegian master, wrote a concerto for piano that was . . ."—she paused—"my mother's triumph at her debut concert in London." Her eyes searched the ceiling. Our eyes followed. Nothing up there but ceiling tile. "For reasons that I shall not go into, my family's fortunes took us to Detroit, then north to dreadful Saginaw, and now here I am in Five Oaks, as your substitute teacher, for today, Thursday, October the eleventh. I believe it will be a good day: all the forecasts coincide. We shall start with your reading lesson. Take out your reading book. I believe it is called *Broad Horizons*, or something along those lines."

Jeannie Vermeesch raised her hand. Miss Ferenczi nodded at her. "Mr. Hibler always starts the day with the Pledge of Allegiance," Jeannie whined.

"Oh, does he? In that case," Miss Ferenczi said, "you must know it *very* well by now, and we certainly need not spend our time on it. No, no allegiance pledging on the premises today, by my reckoning. Not with so much sunlight coming into the room. A pledge does not suit my mood." She glanced at her watch. "Time *is* flying. Take out *Broad Horizons*."

She disappointed us by giving us an ordinary lesson, complete with vocabulary and drills, comprehension questions, and recitation. She didn't seem to care for the material, however.

She sighed every few minutes and rubbed her glasses with a frilly handkerchief that she withdrew, magician-style, from her left sleeve.

After reading we moved on to arithmetic. It was my favorite time of the morning, when the lazy autumn sunlight dazzled its way through ribbons of clouds past the windows on the east side of the classroom and crept across the linoleum floor. On the playground the first group of children, the kindergartners, were running on the quack grass just beyond the monkey bars. We were doing multiplication tables. Miss Ferenczi had made John Wazny stand up at his desk in the front row. He was supposed to go through the tables of six. From where I was sitting, I could smell the Vitalis soaked into John's plastered hair. He was doing fine until he came to six times eleven and six times twelve. "Six times eleven," he said, "is sixty-eight. Six times twelve is . . ." He put his fingers to his head, quickly and secretly sniffed his fingertips, and said, ". . . seventy-two." Then he sat down.

"Fine," Miss Ferenczi said. "Well now. That was very good."

"Miss Ferenczi!" One of the Eddy twins was waving her hand desperately in the air. "Miss Ferenczi! Miss Ferenczi!"

"Yes?"

"John said that six times eleven is sixty-eight and you said he was right!"

"*Did* I?" She gazed at the class with a jolly look breaking across her marionette's face. "Did I say that? Well, what *is* six times eleven?"

"It's sixty-six!"

She nodded. "Yes. So it is. But, and I know some people will not entirely agree with me, at some times it is sixty-eight."

"When? When is it sixty-eight?"

We were all waiting.

"In higher mathematics, which you children do not yet understand, six times eleven can be considered to be sixty-eight." She laughed through her nose. "In higher mathematics numbers are . . . more fluid. The only thing a number does is contain a certain amount of something. Think of water. A cup is not the only way to measure a certain amount of water, is it?" We were staring, shaking our heads. "You could use saucepans or thimbles. In either case, the water *would be the same*. Perhaps," she started again, "it would be better for you to think that six times eleven is sixty-eight only when I am in the room."

"Why is it sixty-eight," Mark Poole asked, "when you're in the room?"

"Because it's more interesting that way," she said, smiling very rapidly behind her blue-tinted glasses. "Besides, I'm your substitute teacher, am I not?" We all nodded. "Well, then, think of six times eleven equals sixty-eight as a substitute fact."

"A substitute fact?"

"Yes." Then she looked at us carefully. "Do you think," she asked, "that anyone is going to be hurt by a substitute fact?"

We looked back at her.

"Will the plants on the windowsill be hurt?" We glanced at them. There were sensitive plants thriving in a green plastic tray, and several wilted ferns in small clay pots. "Your dogs and cats, or your moms and dads?" She waited. "So," she concluded, "what's the problem?"

"But it's wrong," Janice Weber said, "isn't it?"

"What's your name, young lady?"

"Janice Weber."

"And you think it's wrong, Janice?"

"I was just asking."

"Well, all right. You were just asking. I think we've spent enough time on this matter by now, don't you, class? You are free to think what you like. When your teacher, Mr. Hibler, returns, six times eleven will be sixty-six again, you can rest assured. And it will be that for the rest of your lives in Five Oaks. Too bad, eh?" She raised her eyebrows and glinted herself at us. "But for now, it wasn't. So much for that. Let us go on to your assigned problems for today, as painstakingly outlined, I see, in Mr. Hibler's lesson plan. Take out a sheet of paper and write your names on the upper left-hand corner."

For the next half hour we did the rest of our arithmetic problems. We handed them in and then went on to spelling, my worst subject. Spelling always came before lunch. We were taking spelling dictation and looking at the clock. "Thorough," Miss Ferenczi said. "Boundary." She walked in the aisles between the desks, holding the spelling book open and looking down at our papers. "Balcony." I clutched my pencil. Somehow, the way she said those words, they seemed foreign, mis-voweled and mis-consonanted. I stared down at what I had spelled. *Balconie.* I turned the pencil upside down and erased my mistake. *Balconey.* That looked better, but still incorrect. I cursed the world of spelling and tried erasing it again and saw the paper beginning to wear away. *Balkony.* Suddenly I felt a hand on my shoulder.

"I don't like that word either," Miss Ferenczi whispered, bent over, her mouth near my ear. "It's ugly. My feeling is, if you don't like a word, you don't have to use it." She straightened up, leaving behind a slight odor of Clorets.

At lunchtime we went out to get our trays of sloppy joes, peaches in heavy syrup, coconut cookies, and milk, and brought them back to the classroom, where Miss Ferenczi was sitting at the desk, eating a brown sticky thing she had unwrapped from tightly rubber-banded waxed paper. "Miss Ferenczi," I said, raising my hand. "You don't have to eat with us. You can eat with the other teachers. There's a teacher's lounge," I ended up, "next to the principal's office."

"No, thank you," she said. "I prefer it here."

"We've got a room monitor," I said. "Mrs. Eddy." I pointed to where Mrs. Eddy, Joyce and Judy's mother, sat silently at the back of the room, doing her knitting.

"That's fine," Miss Ferenczi said. "But I shall continue to eat here, with you children. I prefer it," she repeated.

"How come?" Wayne Razmer asked without raising his hand.

"I talked to the other teachers before class this morning," Miss Ferenczi said, biting into her brown food. "There was a great rattling of the words for the fewness of the ideas. I didn't care for their brand of hilarity. I don't like ditto-machine jokes."

"Oh," Wayne said.

"What's that you're eating?" Maxine Sylvester asked, twitching her nose. "Is it food?"

"It most certainly *is* food. It's a stuffed fig. I had to drive almost down to Detroit to get it. I also brought some smoked sturgeon. And this," she said, lifting some green leaves out of her lunchbox, "is raw spinach, cleaned this morning."

"Why're you eating raw spinach?" Maxine asked.

"It's good for you," Miss Ferenczi said. "More stimulating than soda pop or smelling salts." I bit into my sloppy joe and stared blankly out the window. An almost invisible moon was faintly silvered in the daytime autumn sky. "As far as food is concerned," Miss Ferenczi was saying, "you have to shuffle the pack. Mix it up. Too many people eat . . . well, never mind."

"Miss Ferenczi," Carol Peterson said, "what are we going to do this afternoon?"

"Well," she said, looking down at Mr. Hibler's lesson plan, "I see that your teacher, Mr. Hibler, has you scheduled for a unit on the Egyptians." Carol groaned. "Yessss," Miss Ferenczi continued, "that is what we will do: the Egyptians. A remarkable people. Almost as remarkable as the Americans. But not quite." She lowered her head, did her quick smile, and went back to eating her spinach.

After noon recess we came back into the classroom and saw that Miss Ferenczi had drawn a pyramid on the blackboard close to her oak tree. Some of us who had been playing baseball were messing around in the back of the room, dropping the bats and gloves into the playground box, and Ray Schontzeler had just slugged me when I heard Miss Ferenczi's high-pitched voice, quavering with emotions. "Boys," she said, "come to order right this minute and take your seats. I do not wish to waste a minute of class time. Take out your geography books." We trudged to our desks and, still sweating, pulled out *Distant Lands and Their People*. "Turn to page forty-two." She waited for thirty seconds, then looked over at Kelly Munger. "Young man," she said, "why are you still fossicking in your desk?"

Kelly looked as if his foot had been stepped on. "Why am I what?"

"Why are you . . . burrowing in your desk like that?"

"I'm lookin' for the book, Miss Ferenczi."

Bobby Kryzanowicz, the faultless brownnoser who sat in the first row by choice, softly said, "His name is Kelly Munger. He can't ever find his stuff. He always does that."

"I don't care what his name is, especially after lunch," Miss Ferenczi said. *"Where is your book?"*

71

"I just found it." Kelly was peering into his desk and with both hands pulled at the book, shoveling along in front of it several pencils and crayons, which fell into his lap and then to the floor.

"I hate a mess," Miss Ferenczi said. "I hate a mess in a desk or a mind. It's . . . unsanitary. You wouldn't want your house at home to look like your desk at school, now, would you?" She didn't wait for an answer. "I should think not. A house at home should be as neat as human hands can make it. What were we talking about? Egypt. Page forty-two. I note from Mr. Hibler's lesson plan that you have been discussing the modes of Egyptian irrigation. Interesting, in my view, but not so interesting as what we are about to cover. The pyramids, and Egyptian slave labor. A plus on one side, a minus on the other." We had our books open to page forty-two, where there was a picture of a pyramid, but Miss Ferenczi wasn't looking at the book. Instead, she was staring at some object just outside the window.

"Pyramids," Miss Ferenczi said, still looking past the window. "I want you to think about pyramids. And what was inside. The bodies of the pharaohs, of course, and their attendant treasures. Scrolls. Perhaps," Miss Ferenczi said, her face gleeful but unsmiling, "these scrolls were novels for the pharaohs, helping them to pass the time in their long voyage through the centuries. But then, I am joking." I was looking at the lines on Miss Ferenczi's skin. "Pyramids," Miss Ferenczi went on, "were the repositories of special cosmic powers. The nature of a pyramid is to guide cosmic energy forces into a concentrated point. The Egyptians knew that; we have generally forgotten it. Did you know," she asked, walking to the side of the room so that she was standing by the coat closet, "that George Washington had Egyptian blood, from his grandmother? Certain features of the Constitution of the United States are notable for their Egyptian ideas."

Without glancing down at the book, she began to talk about the movement of souls in Egyptian religion. She said that when people die, their souls return to Earth in the form of carpenter ants or walnut trees, depending on how they behaved—"well or ill"—in life. She said that the Egyptians believed that people act the way they do because of magnetism produced by tidal forces in the solar system, forces produced by the sun and by its "planetary ally," Jupiter. Jupiter, she said, was a planet, as we had been told, but had "certain properties of stars." She was speaking very fast. She said that the Egyptians were great explorers and conquerors. She said that the greatest of all the conquerors, Genghis Khan, had had forty horses and forty young women killed on the site of his grave. We listened. No one tried to stop her. "I myself have been in Egypt," she said, "and have witnessed much dust and many brutalities." She said that an old man in Egypt who worked for a circus had personally shown her an animal in a cage, a monster, half bird and half lion. She said that this monster was called a gryphon and that she had heard about them but never seen them until she traveled to the outskirts of Cairo. She wrote the word out on the blackboard in large capital letters: GRYPHON. She said that Egyptian astronomers had discovered the planet Saturn but had not seen its rings. She said that the Egyptians were the first to discover that dogs, when they are ill, will not drink from rivers, but wait for rain, and hold their jaws open to catch it.

"She lies."

We were on the school bus home. I was sitting next to Carl Whiteside, who had bad breath and a huge collection of marbles. We were arguing. Carl thought she was lying. I said she wasn't, probably.

"I didn't believe that stuff about the bird," Carl said, "and what she told us about the pyramids? I didn't believe that, either. She didn't know what she was talking about."

"Oh yeah?" I had liked her. She was strange. I thought I could nail him. "If she was lying," I said, "what'd she say that was a lie?"

"Six times eleven isn't sixty-eight. It isn't ever. It's sixty-six, I know for a fact."

"She said so. She admitted it. What else did she lie about?"

"I don't know," he said. "Stuff."

"What stuff?"

"Well." He swung his legs back and forth. "You ever see an animal that was half lion and half bird?" He crossed his arms. "It sounded real fakey to me."

"It could happen," I said. I had to improvise, to outrage him. "I read in this newspaper my mom bought in the IGA about this scientist, this mad scientist in the Swiss Alps, and he's been putting genes and chromosomes and stuff together in test tubes, and he combined a human being and a hamster." I waited, for effect. "It's called a humster."

"You never." Carl was staring at me, his mouth open, his terrible bad breath making its way toward me. "What newspaper was it?"

"*The National Enquirer*," I said, "that they sell next to the cash registers." When I saw his look of recognition, I knew I had him. "And this mad scientist," I said, "his name was, um, Dr. Frankenbush." I realized belatedly that this name was a mistake and waited for Carl to notice its resemblance to the name of the other famous mad master of permutations, but he only sat there.

"A man and a hamster?" He was staring at me, squinting, his mouth opening in distaste. "Jeez. What'd it look like?"

When the bus reached my stop, I took off down our dirt road and ran up through the backyard, kicking the tire swing for good luck. I dropped my books on the back steps so I could hug and kiss our dog, Mr. Selby. Then I hurried inside. I could smell brussels sprouts cooking, my unfavorite vegetable. My mother was washing other vegetables in the kitchen sink, and my baby brother was hollering in his yellow playpen on the kitchen floor.

"Hi, Mom," I said, hopping around the playpen to kiss her. "Guess what?"

"I have no idea."

"We had this substitute today, Miss Ferenczi, and I'd never seen her before, and she had all these stories and ideas and stuff."

"Well. That's good." My mother looked out the window in front of the sink, her eyes on the pine woods west of our house. That time of the afternoon her skin always looked so white to me. Strangers always said my mother looked like Betty Crocker, framed by the giant spoon on the side of the Bisquick box. "Listen, Tommy," she said. "Would you please go upstairs and pick your clothes off the floor in the bathroom, and then go outside to the shed and put the shovel and ax away that your father left outside this morning?"

"She said that six times eleven was sometimes sixty-eight!" I said. "And she said she once saw a monster that was half lion and half bird." I waited. "In Egypt."

"Did you hear me?" my mother asked, raising her arm to wipe her forehead with the back of her hand. "You have chores to do."

"I know," I said. "I was just telling you about the substitute."

"It's very interesting," my mother said, quickly glancing down at me, "and we can talk about it later when your father gets home. But right now you have some work to do."

"Okay, Mom." I took a cookie out of the jar on the counter and was about to go outside when I had a thought. I ran into the living room, pulled out a dictionary next to the TV stand, and opened it to the Gs. After five minutes I found it. *Gryphon*: variant of griffin. *Griffin*: "a fabulous beast with the head and wings of an eagle and the body of a lion." Fabulous was right. I shouted with triumph and ran outside to put my father's tools in their proper places.

Miss Ferenczi was back the next day, slightly altered. She had pulled her hair down and twisted it into pigtails, with red rubber bands holding them tight one inch from the ends. She was wearing a green blouse and pink scarf, making her difficult to look at for a full class day. This time there was no pretense of doing a reading lesson or moving on to arithmetic. As soon as the bell rang, she simply began to talk.

She talked for forty minutes straight. There seemed to be less connection between her ideas, but the ideas themselves were, as the dictionary would say, fabulous. She said she had heard of a huge jewel, in what she called the antipodes, that was so brilliant that when light shone into it at a certain angle it would blind whoever was looking at its center. She said the biggest diamond in the world was cursed and had killed everyone who owned it, and that by a trick of fate it was called the Hope Diamond. Diamonds are magic, she said, and this is why women wear them on their fingers, as a sign of the magic of womanhood. Men have strength, Miss Ferenczi said, but no true magic. That is why men fall in love with women but women do not fall in love with men: they just love being loved. George Washington had died because of a mistake he made about a diamond. Washington was not the first *true* president, but she didn't say who was. In some places in the world, she said, men and women still live in the trees and eat monkeys for breakfast. Their doctors are magicians. At the bottom of the sea are creatures thin as pancakes who have never been studied by scientists because when you take them up to air, the fish explode.

There was not a sound in the classroom, except for Miss Ferenczi's voice, and Donna DeShano's coughing. No one even went to the bathroom.

Beethoven, she said, had not been deaf; it was a trick to make himself famous, and it worked. As she talked, Miss Ferenczi's pigtails swung back and forth. There are trees in the world, she said, that eat meat: their leaves are sticky and close up on bugs like hands. She lifted her hands and brought them together, palm to palm. Venus, which most people think is the next closest planet to the sun, is not always closer, and, besides, it is the planet of greatest mystery because of its thick cloud cover. "I know what lies underneath those clouds," Miss Ferenczi said, and waited. After the silence, she said, "Angels. Angels live under those clouds." She said that angels were not invisible to everyone and were in fact smarter than most people. They did not dress in robes as was often claimed but instead wore formal evening clothes, as if they were about to attend a concert. Often angels *do* attend concerts and sit in the aisles, where, she said, most people pay no attention to them. She said the most terrible angel had the shape of the Sphinx. "There is no running away from that one," she said. She said that unquenchable fires burn just under the surface of the earth in Ohio, and that the baby Mozart fainted dead away in his cradle when he first heard the sound of a trumpet. She said that someone named Narzim al Harrardim was the greatest writer who ever lived. She said that planets control behavior, and anyone conceived during a solar eclipse would be born with webbed feet.

"I know you children like to hear these things," she said, "these secrets, and that is why I am telling you all this." We nodded. It was better than doing comprehension questions for the readings in *Broad Horizons*.

"I will tell you one more story," she said, "and then we will have to do arithmetic." She leaned over, and her voice grew soft. "There is no death," she said. "You must never be afraid. Never. That which is, cannot die. It will change into different earthly and unearthly elements, but I know this as sure as I stand here in front of you, and I swear it: you must not be afraid. I have seen this truth with these eyes. I know it because in a dream God kissed me. Here." And she pointed with her right index finger to the side of her head, below the mouth where the vertical lines were carved into her skin.

Absentmindedly we all did our arithmetic problems. At recess the class was out on the playground, but no one was playing. We were all standing in small groups, talking about Miss Ferenczi. We didn't know if she was crazy, or what. I looked out beyond the playground, at the rusted cars piled in a small heap behind a clump of sumac, and I wanted to see shapes there, approaching me.

On the way home, Carl sat next to me again. He didn't say much, and I didn't either. At last he turned to me. "You know what she said about the leaves that close up on bugs?"

"Huh?"

"The leaves," Carl insisted. "The meat-eating plants. I know it's true. I saw it on television. The leaves have this icky glue that the plants have got smeared all over them and the insects can't get off 'cause they're stuck. I saw it." He seemed demoralized. "She's tellin' the truth."

"Yeah."

"You think she's seen all those angels?"

I shrugged.

"I don't think she has," Carl informed me. "I think she made that part up."

"There's a tree," I suddenly said. I was looking out the window at the farms along County Road H. I knew every barn, every broken windmill, every fence, every anhydrous ammonia tank, by heart. "There's a tree that's . . . that I've seen . . ."

"Don't you try to do it," Carl said. "You'll just sound like a jerk."

I kissed my mother. She was standing in front of the stove. "How was your day?" she asked.

"Fine."

"Did you have Miss Ferenczi again?"

"Yeah."

"Well?"

"She was fine. Mom," I asked, "can I go to my room?"

"No," she said, "not until you've gone out to the vegetable garden and picked me a few tomatoes." She glanced at the sky. "I think it's going to rain. Skedaddle and do it now. Then you come back inside and watch your brother for a few minutes while I go upstairs. I need to clean up before dinner." She looked down at me. "You're looking a little pale, Tommy." She

79

touched the back of her hand to my forehead and I felt her diamond ring against my skin. "Do you feel all right?"

"I'm fine," I said, and went out to pick the tomatoes.

Coughing mutedly, Mr. Hibler was back the next day, slipping lozenges into his mouth when his back was turned at forty-five-minute intervals and asking us how much of his prepared lesson plan Miss Ferenczi had followed. Edith Atwater took the responsibility for the class of explaining to Mr. Hibler that the substitute hadn't always done exactly what he, Mr. Hibler, would have done, but we had worked hard even though she talked a lot. About what? he asked. All kinds of things, Edith said. I sort of forgot. To our relief, Mr. Hibler seemed not at all interested in what Miss Ferenczi had said to fill the day. He probably thought it was woman's talk: unserious and not suited for school. It was enough that he had a pile of arithmetic problems from us to correct.

For the next month, the sumac turned a distracting red in the field, and the sun traveled toward the southern sky, so that its rays reached Mr. Hibler's Halloween display on the bulletin board in the back of the room, fading the pumpkin-head scarecrow from orange to tan. Every three days I measured how much farther the sun had moved toward the southern horizon by making small marks with my black Crayola on the north wall, ant-sized marks only I knew were there.

And then in early December, four days after the first permanent snowfall, she appeared again in our classroom. The minute she came in the door, I felt my heart begin to pound. Once again, she was different: this time, her hair hung straight down and seemed hardly to have been combed. She hadn't brought her lunchbox with her, but she was carrying what seemed to be a small box. She greeted all of us and talked about the weather. Donna DeShano had to remind her to take her overcoat off.

When the bell to start the day finally rang, Miss Ferenczi looked out at all of us and said, "Children, I have enjoyed your company in the past, and today I am going to reward you." She held up the small box. "Do you know what this is?" She waited. "Of course you don't. It is a tarot pack."

Edith Atwater raised her hand. "What's a tarot pack, Miss Ferenczi?"

"It is used to tell fortunes," she said. "And that is what I shall do this morning. I shall tell your fortunes, as I have been taught to do."

"What's fortune?" Bobby Kryzanowicz asked.

"The future, young man. I shall tell you what your future will be. I can't do your whole future, of course. I shall have to limit myself to the five-card system, the wands, cups, swords, pentacles, and the higher arcanes. Now who wants to be first?"

There was a long silence. Then Carol Peterson raised her hand.

"All right," Miss Ferenczi said. She divided the pack into five smaller packs and walked back to Carol's desk, in front of mine. "Pick one card from each one of these packs," she said. I saw that Carol had a four of cups and a six of swords, but I couldn't see the other cards. Miss Ferenczi studied the cards on Carol's desk for a minute. "Not bad," she said. "I do not see much higher education. Probably an early marriage. Many children. There's something bleak and dreary here, but I can't tell what. Perhaps just the tasks of a housewife life. I think you'll do very well, for the most part." She smiled at Carol, a smile with a certain lack of interest. "Who wants to be next?"

Carl Whiteside raised his hand slowly.

"Yes," Miss Ferenczi said, "let's do a boy." She walked over to where Carl sat. After he picked his five cards, she gazed at them for a long time. "Travel," she said. "Much distant travel. You might go into the army. Not too much romantic interest here. A late marriage, if at all. But the sun in your major arcana, that's a very good card." She giggled. "You'll have a happy life."

Next I raised my hand. She told me my future. She did the same with Bobby Kryzanowicz, Kelly Munger, Edith Atwater, and Kim Foor. Then she came to Wayne Razmer. He picked his five cards, and I could see that the death card was one of them.

"What's your name?" Miss Ferenczi asked.

"Wayne."

"Well, Wayne," she said, "you will undergo a great meta-morphosis, a change, before you become an adult. Your earthly element will no doubt leap higher, because you seem to be a sweet boy. This card, this nine of swords, tells me of suffering and desolation. And this ten of wands, well, that's a heavy load."

"What about this one?" Wayne pointed at the death card.

"It means, my sweet, that you will die soon." She gathered up the cards. We were all looking at Wayne. "But do not fear," she said. "It is not really death. Just change. Out of your earthly shape." She put the cards on Mr. Hibler's desk. "And now, let's do some arithmetic."

At lunchtime Wayne went to Mr. Faegre, the principal, and informed him of what Miss Ferenczi had done. During the noon recess, we saw Miss Ferenczi drive out of the parking lot in her rusting green Rambler American. I stood under the slide, listening to the other kids coasting down and landing in the little depressive bowls at the bottom. I was kicking stones and tugging at my hair right up to the moment when I saw

Wayne come out to the playground. He smiled, the dead fool, and with the fingers of his right hand he was showing everyone how he had told on Miss Ferenczi.

I made my way toward Wayne, pushing myself past two girls from another class. He was watching me with his little pinhead eyes.

"You told," I shouted at him. "She was just kidding."

"She shouldn't have," he shouted back. "We were supposed to be doing arithmetic."

"She just scared you," I said. "You're a chicken. You're a chicken, Wayne. You are. Scared of a little card," I singsonged.

Wayne fell at me, his two fists hammering down on my nose. I gave him a good one in the stomach and then I tried for his head. Aiming my fist, I saw that he was crying. I slugged him.

"She was right," I yelled. "She was always right! She told the truth!" Other kids were whooping. "You were just scared, that's all!"

And then large hands pulled at us, and it was my turn to speak to Mr. Faegre.

In the afternoon Miss Ferenczi was gone, and my nose was stuffed with cotton clotted with blood, and my lip had swelled, and our class had been combined with Mrs. Mantei's sixth-grade class for a crowded afternoon science unit on insect life in ditches and swamps. I knew where Mrs. Mantei lived: she had a new house trailer just down the road from us, at the Clearwater Park. She was no mystery. Somehow she and Mr. Bodine, the other fourth-grade teacher, had managed to fit forty-five desks into the room. Kelly Munger asked if Miss Ferenczi had been arrested, and Mrs. Mantei said no, of course not. All that afternoon, until the buses came to pick us up, we learned about field crickets and two-striped grasshoppers, water bugs, cicadas, mosquitoes, flies, and moths. We learned about insects' hard outer shell, the exoskeleton, and the usual parts of the mouth, including the labrum, mandible, maxilla, and glossa. We learned about compound eyes, and the four-stage metamorphosis from egg to larva to pupa to adult. We learned something, but not much, about mating. Mrs. Mantei drew, very skillfully, the internal anatomy of the grasshopper on the blackboard. We learned about the dance of the honeybee, directing other bees in the hive to pollen. We found out about which insects were pests to man, and which were not. On lined white pieces of paper we made lists of insects we might actually see, then a list of insects too small to be clearly visible, such as fleas; Mrs. Mantei said that our assignment would be to memorize these lists for the next day, when Mr. Hibler would certainly return and test us on our knowledge.

FELLOWSHIP

Franz Kafka

We are five friends; one day we came out of a house one after the other; first, one came and placed himself beside the gate, then the second came, or rather he glided through the gate like a little ball of quicksilver, and placed himself near the first one, then came the third, then the fourth, then the fifth. Finally we all stood in a row. People began to notice us; they pointed at us and said: Those five just came out of that house. Since then we have been living together; it would be a peaceful life if it weren't for a sixth one continually trying to interfere. He doesn't do us any harm, but he annoys us, and that is harm enough; why does he intrude where he is not wanted? We don't know him and don't want him to join us. There was a time, of course, when the five of us did not know one another, either; and it could be said that we still don't know one another, but what is possible and can be tolerated by the five of us is not possible and cannot be tolerated with this sixth one. In any case, we are five and don't want to be six. And what is the point of this continual being together anyhow? It is also pointless for the five of us, but here we are together and will remain together; a new combination, however, we do not want, just because of our experiences. But how is one to make all this clear to the sixth one? Long explanations would almost amount to accepting him in our circle, so we prefer not to explain and not to accept him. No matter how he pouts his lips we push him away with our elbows, but however much we push him away, back he comes.

APPROXIMATIONS

Mona Simpson

In my family, there were always two people. First, my mother and father. Carol and John.

They danced. Hundreds of evenings at hundreds of parties in their twenties. A thousand times between songs her eyes completely closed when she leaned against him. He looked down at the top of her head; her part gleamed white, under and between the dark hair. He rubbed her back, trying to rouse her, but she became indistinct, blurring against his jacket. He hugged her imperceptibly closer, moving his hand in slower circles on her back, but when he talked it was to someone else over her head. He closed a big hand on her ear.

How do I know this? I don't. But there was a black-and-white snapshot with my father staring at someone outside the frame. I was looking at the picture when, for some reason, I asked my mother where he was.

I was young, only four years old, and I had no memories of my father. I must have been repeating a question someone else had asked me. My mother was ironing. It was 1960 and all her summer clothes were seersucker and cotton. Her hands stalled over the iron when I asked the question.

"He's gone," she said, not looking at me. The windows were open. A string of hummingbirds moved on the lilac bush outside. "But," she said, gathering her cheeks, "he'll be coming back."

"When?"

For a moment, her mouth wavered, but then her chin snapped back into a straight line and she pushed the iron over the perforated pink and white fabric again.

"I don't know," she said.

So we waited, without mentioning it, for my father. In the meantime, we got used to living alone. Just the two of us.

Other people asked me questions.

"Any news from your dad?"

"I don't know."

"You must miss him." Other mothers got maternal, pulling me close to their soft, aproned bellies.

For a moment, but only for a moment, I'd let my eyes close. Then I jerked away. "No," I said.

Saturday nights, we went ice-skating. We wore skin-colored tights and matching short dresses made out of stretch fabric. We skated in tight concentrated figures, our necks bent like horses', following the lines of an 8. Then, when the PA system started up, we broke into free skating, wild around the rink. My mother skated up behind me and caught me at the waist.

"This is how you really lose the pounds," she called, slapping her thigh, "skating fast."

I was always behind. Jerry, the pro, did a T-stop to impress my mother, shaving a comet of ice into the air. They skated around together and I had to slow down to wipe the melting water from my face.

When the music stopped, my mother pulled me over to the barrier, where we ran our skate tips into the soft wood. She pointed up to the rows of empty seats. They were maroon, with the plush worn down in the centers.

"See, when you're older, you can bring a boy you're dating here to see you skate. He can watch and think, hey, she's not just another pretty girl, she can really do something."

She peered into my face with a slanted gaze as if, through a crack, she could see what I'd become.

Taking the skates off, on the bench, was all joy. You could walk without carrying your own weight. Your feet and ankles were pure air. The floors were carpeted with rubber mats, red and black, like a checkerboard. In regular shoes, we walked like saints on clouds. The high-domed arena was always cold.

The first time we heard from my father was 1963 in the middle of winter. We got a long distance phone call from Las Vegas and it was him.

"We're going to Disneyland!" my mother said, lifting her eyebrows and covering the mouthpiece with her hand.

Into the phone, she said she'd take me out of school. We'd fly to Las Vegas and then the three of us would drive west to Disneyland. I didn't recognize his voice when my mother held out the receiver.

"Hello, Melinda. This is Daddy."

I shrugged at my mother and wouldn't take the phone. "You'll know him when you see him," she whispered.

We waited three days for our summer linen dresses to be dry-cleaned. "It's going to be *hot*," my mother warned.

"Scorching," she added with a smile. It was snowing dry powder when we left Illinois. We only saw white outside the airplane window. Halfway there, we changed in the tiny bathroom, from our winter coats to sleeveless dresses and patent leather thongs. It was still cool in the plane but my mother promised it would be hot on the ground.

It was. The air was swirling with dirt. A woman walked across the airport lobby with a scarf tied around her chest; it trailed behind her, coasting on air.

My mother spotted my father in the crowd, and we all pretended I recognized him too. He looked like an ordinary man. His hair was balding in a small circle. He wore tight black slacks, a brown jacket, and black leather, slip-on shoes. His chin stuck out from his face, giving him an eager look.

He had a car parked outside and my mother got into the front seat with him. We passed hotels with bright blue swimming pools and the brown tinge of the sky hung over the water, like a line of dirt on the rim of a sleeve.

My father's apartment was in a pink stucco building. When we walked up with our suitcases, his three roommates were crowded on the porch, leaning on the iron banister. They wore white V-neck T-shirts and thick dark hair pressed out from under them. I hadn't seen men dressed like that before.

"He told us you had long blond hair."

"You look like your dad."

"She's prettier than her dad."

When my father smiled, the gaps between his teeth made him look unintentionally sad, like a jack-o'-lantern. He looked down and I felt he was proud of me. He touched my hair. I loved him blindly, the feeling darkening over everything, but it passed.

My mother stepped up to the porch. "Don't you want to introduce me to your friends, too?"

My father introduced each man separately and each man smiled. Then my father gave me a present: a package of six different-colored cotton headbands. I held it and didn't tear the cellophane open.

My father worked as a waiter in a hotel restaurant. We had dinner there, eating slowly while he worked, watching him balance dishes on the inside of his arm. He sat down with us while my mother was sipping her coffee. He crossed one leg over the other, smoking luxuriously. My mother leaned closer and whispered in my ear.

"When are we going to Disneyland?" I asked, blankly, saying what she said to say but somehow knowing it was wrong.

My father didn't answer me. He looked at my mother and put out his cigarette. That night in the apartment, they fought. My father's roommates closed the doors to their rooms.

"So, when are we going," my mother asked gamely, crossing one leg over the other on a dinette chair.

His shoulders sloped down. "You were late," he said finally. "You were supposed to be here Monday. When you didn't come, I lost the money I'd saved."

"In three days, how? How could you do that?"

"On the tables."

"You, you can't do this to her," my mother said, her voice gathering like a wave.

They sent me outside to the porch. I heard everything, even their breath, through the screen door. There was a box of matches on the ground and I lit them, one by one, scratching them against the concrete and then dropping them in the dirt when the flames came too close to my fingers. Finally it was quiet. My father came out and opened the screen door and I went in.

They set up the living room couch as a bed for me. They both undressed in my father's bedroom. He pulled off his T-shirt and sat on the bed to untie his shoes. My mother looked back at me, over her shoulder, while she unzipped her dress. Finally, she closed the door.

The next morning my father and I got up before my mother. We went to the hotel coffee shop and sat on stools at the counter. I was afraid to ask for anything; I said I wasn't hungry. My father ordered a soft-boiled egg for himself. His eyes caught on the uniformed waitress, the coffeepot tilting from her hand, a purse on the other end of the counter. The egg came in a white coffee cup. He chopped it with the edge of a spoon, asking me if I'd ever tasted a four-minute egg. I ate a spoonful and I loved it. No other egg was ever so good. I told my father how good it was hoping we could share it. But he slid the whole cup down, the spoon in it, without looking at me and signaled the waitress for another egg.

Walking back to the apartment, he kicked sand into the air. There were no lawns in front of the parked trailers, but the sand was raked and bordered with rows of rocks. My father's black slip-on shoes were scuffed. He was holding my hand but not looking at me.

"So we'll go to Disneyland next trip," he said.

"When?"

Suddenly, I wanted dates and plans and the name of a month, not to see Disneyland but to see him. Taking long steps, trying to match his pace, I wanted to say that I didn't care about Disneyland. I dared myself to talk, after one more, two more, three more steps, all the way to the apartment. But I never said it. All I did was hold his hand tighter and tighter.

"I don't know," he said, letting my hand drop when we came to the steps in front of his apartment.

On the plane home, I was holding the package of headbands in my lap, tracing them through the cellophane. My mother turned away and looked out the window.

"I work," she said finally. "I pay for your school and your books and your skates and your lessons. *And*," she said in a louder whisper, "I pay the rent."

She picked up the package of headbands and then dropped it back on my lap.

"A seventy-nine-cent package of headbands."

It wasn't fair and I knew it.

The next year my mother went back to Las Vegas without me. She and Jerry, the ice-skating pro, got married. She came back without any pictures of the wedding and Jerry moved in with us.

She said she didn't want to bother with a big wedding since it was her second marriage. She wore a dress she already had.

My mother and I spent all that summer in the arena, where Jerry ran an ice-skating school. All day long the air conditioners hummed like the inside of a refrigerator. Inside the door of my locker was a picture of Peggy Fleming. Inside my mother's was Sonja Henie. In the main office, there were framed pictures of Jerry during his days with Holiday on Ice and the Ice Capades. In them, he didn't look like himself. He had short bristly hair and a glamorous smile. His dark figure slithered backward, his arms pointing to two corners of the photograph. The lighting was yellow and false. In one of the pictures it was snowing.

We practiced all summer for the big show in August. The theme was the calendar; the chorus changed from December angels to April bunnies and May tulips. I couldn't get the quick turns in time with the older girls, so I was taken out of the chorus and given a role of my own. After the Easter number was over and the skaters in bunny costumes crowded backstage, I skated fast around the rink, blowing kisses. A second later, the Zamboni came out to clear the ice. I stood in back before my turn, terrified to go out too early or too late, with the velvet curtain bunched in my hand.

My mother came up behind me every show and gave me a push, saying "now, go" at the right time. I skated completely by instinct. I couldn't see. My eyes blurred under the strong spotlight. But one night, during the Easter dance, my mother was near the stage exit, laughing with Jerry. She kept trying to bend down to tie her laces and he pulled her up, kissing her. Finally, looking over his shoulder, she saw me and quickly mouthed "go." I went out then but it was too late. I heard the Zamboni growling behind me. I tried to run, forgetting how to skate, and fell forward, flat on the ice. My hands burned when I hurried up behind the moving spotlight and I saw that I'd torn my tights. The edges of the hole on my knee were ragged with blood.

I sat down on the ice backstage while the music for my mother's number started up. I knew it by heart. Jerry led my mother in an elementary waltz. She glinted along the ice, shifting her weight from leg to bent leg. Her skates slid out from her body. She was heavier than she had once been. She swayed, moving her head to glance off the eyes of the crowd. Under the slow spotlight, she twirled inside the box of Jerry's arms.

I quit skating after that. When my mother and Jerry went to the rink I stayed home or went out to play with the other kids in the neighborhood. The next year I joined the Girl Scout troop.

Eventually, my mother stopped taking lessons, too. Then Jerry went to the rink himself every day, like any other man going to a job.

One Saturday, there was a father/daughter breakfast sponsored by my Girl Scout troop. I must have told my mother about it. But by the time the day came, I'd forgotten and I was all dressed in my play clothes to go outside. I was out the front door when my mother caught me.

"Melinda."

"What?"

"Where are you going?"

"The end of the block."

"Don't you remember your Girl Scout breakfast? You have to go in and change."

I didn't want to go. I was already on the driveway, straddling my bike.

"I don't feel like going to that. I'd rather play."

My mother was wearing her housecoat, but she came outside anyway, holding it closed with one hand over her chest.

"He took the day off and he's in there now getting dressed. Now, come on. Go in and put something on."

"No," I said, "I don't want to."

"Won't you do this for me?" she whispered. "He wants to *adopt* you."

We stood there a minute and then the screen door opened.

"Let her go, Carol. She doesn't have to go if she doesn't want to go. It's up to her."

Jerry was standing in the doorway, all dressed up. His hair was combed down and wet from just taking a shower. He was wearing a white turtleneck sweater and a paisley ascot. I felt sorry for him, looking serious and dressed up like that, and I wanted to change my mind and go in but I thought it was too late and I flew off on my bike. None of the other fathers would be wearing ascots anyway, I was thinking.

My father called again when I was ten, to say he wanted to take me to Disneyland. He said he was living in Reno, Nevada, with a new wife. He and my mother bickered a long time on the phone. He wanted to send a plane ticket for me to come alone. My mother said either both of us went or neither. She said she was afraid he would kidnap me. She held out. Finally, they agreed he'd send the money for two tickets.

Around this time, my mother always told me her dreams, which were about things she wanted. A pale blue Lincoln Continental with a cream-colored interior. A swimming pool with night lights and a redwood fence around the yard. A house with a gazebo you couldn't see from the road.

She had already stopped telling Jerry the things she wanted because he tried to get them for her and he made mistakes. He approximated. He bought her the wrong kind of record player for Christmas and he got a dull gold Cadillac, a used car, for her birthday.

Before we went to California, my mother read about something she wanted. A New Sony Portable Color Television. A jewel. She wanted a white one, she was sure it came in white. In the short magazine article she'd clipped out, it said the TVs were available only in Japan until early 1967, next year, but my mother was sure that by the time we went, they would be all over California.

Jerry took us to the airport and he was quiet while we checked on our luggage. When we got onto the plane, we forgot about him. We made plans to get my father to buy us the new Sony. It was this trip's Disneyland. We'd either win it or lose it depending on how we played.

At the airport in Los Angeles, we met Velma, my father's new wife. She was a good ten years older and rich; her fingers were full of jewelry and she had on a brown fur coat.

This trip there was no struggle. We went straight to Disneyland. We stayed in the Disneyland Hotel. The four of us went through Disneyland like a rake. There was nothing we didn't see. We ate at restaurants. We bought souvenirs.

But knowing the real purpose of our trip made talking to my father complicated. As I watched my mother laugh with him I was never sure if it was a real laugh, for pleasure, or if it was work, to get our TV. My father seemed sad and a little bumbling. With everyone else around, my father and I didn't talk much.

"How's school?" he asked, walking to the Matterhorn.

"Fine," I said, "I like it."

"That's good," he said.

Our conversations were always like that. It was like lighting single matches.

And I was getting nervous. We were leaving in a day and nothing was being done about the new Sony. The last night, Velma suggested that I meet my father downstairs in the lobby before dinner, so the two of us could talk alone. In our room, my mother brushed my hair out in a fan across my back.

I was nervous. I didn't know what to say to my father.

My mother knew. "See if you can get him to buy the TV," she said. "I bet they've got one for sale right nearby."

I said I hadn't seen any in the stores.

"I think I saw one," she said, winking, "a white one."

"What should I do?" I knew I had to learn everything.

"Tell him you're saving up for it. He'll probably just buy it for you." My mother wasn't nervous. "Suck in your cheeks," she said, brushing glitter on my face. She was having fun.

I didn't want to leave the room. But my mother gave me a short push and I went slowly down the stairs. I tried to remember everything she told me. *Chin up. Smile. Brush your hair back. Say you're saving for it. Suck in your cheeks.* It seemed I was on the verge of losing one of two things I badly wanted. With each step it seemed I was choosing.

I saw my father's back first. He was standing by the candy counter. Whenever I saw my father I went through a series of gradual adjustments, like when you step out of the ice rink, in summer, and feel the warm air. I had to focus my vision down from an idea as vague as a color, to him. He was almost bald. The way his chin shot out made him always look eager. He was buying a roll of Life Savers.

"Would you like anything?" he asked, seeing me and tilting his head to indicate the rows of candy arranged on the counter.

I thought for a wild moment. I could give up the plan, smile and say yes. Yes I want a candy bar. Two candy bars. He'd buy me two of the best candy bars there. I could stand and eat them sloppily, all the while gazing up at my father. If I smiled, he would smile. He would bend down and dab the chocolate from my mouth with a handkerchief moist with his own saliva.

But I didn't say yes, because I knew it would end. I knew I'd remember my father's face, soft on mine, next year when no letters came. I would hate my best memory because it would prove that my father could fake love or that love could end or, worst of all, that love was not powerful enough to change a life, his life.

"No," I said, "I'm saving up my money."

"What?" he said, smiling down at me. He was unraveling the paper from his Life Savers.

I gulped. "I'm saving my money for a new Sony portable color television," I said.

He scanned the drugstore for a moment. I think we both knew he was relinquishing me to my mother.

"Oh," he said finally, nodding.

We didn't get the Sony. On the way home, neither of us mentioned it. And when the plane landed, we didn't call Jerry. We took a taxi from the airport. When we got home, my mother collapsed on the blue-green couch and looked around the room disapprovingly. The suitcases were scattered on the floor.

"You didn't say one big word the whole time we were there," she said. "Here, you're clever. You should hear yourself kidding around with Jerry. You say three syllable words and . . . There, you didn't say one smart thing in front of him. Let me tell you, you sounded dumb."

She imitated a dumb person, stretching her eyes wide open and puffing air into her cheeks.

She sighed. "Go out and play," she said. "Go out and play with your friends."

But I just stood there looking at her. She got worse. She kicked off her shoes. She began throwing pillows from the couch onto the floor.

"Not one big word. The whole time we were there," she said.

"And you didn't smile. Here, you're sharp, you're animate. There you slumped. You looked down. You really just looked ordinary. Like any other kid around here. Well, it's a good thing we're back because I can see now this is just where you belong. With all the mill workers' kids. Well, here we are. Good."

She was still yelling when I walked out the door. Then I did something I'd never done before. I walked down to the end of our road and I hitchhiked. I got picked up by a lady who lived two blocks away. I told her I was going to the arena.

From the lobby I saw Jerry on the ice. I ran downstairs to my mother's locker and sat alone, lacing up skates. I ran up the hall on my skate points and I ran onto the ice fast, my arms straight out to the sides. I went flying toward Jerry.

He was bending over a woman's shoulders, steering her into a figure eight.

A second later he saw me and I was in his arms, breathing against the wool of his sweater. He put a hand over my ear and told his student something I couldn't understand.

A few seconds later, when I pulled myself away, the student was gone. I stopped crying and then there was nothing to do. We were alone on the ice.

I looked up at Jerry; it was different than with my father. I couldn't bury my face in Jerry's sweater and forget the world. I stood there nervously. Jerry was still Jerry, standing in front of me shyly, a man I didn't know. My father was gone for good and here was Jerry, just another man in the world, who had nothing to do with me.

"Would you like me to teach you to do loops?" he asked quietly.

I couldn't say no because of how he looked, standing there with his hands in his pockets.

I glanced up at the empty stands around us. I was tired. And cold. Jerry started skating in tight, precise loops. I looked down at the lines he was making on the ice.

"I'll try," I said, beginning to follow them.

THE BET

Anton Chekhov

1

It was a dark autumn night. The old banker was walking up and down his study and remembering how, fifteen years before, he had given a party one autumn evening. There had been many clever men there, and there had been interesting conversations. Among other things they had talked of capital punishment. The majority of the guests, among whom were many journalists and intellectual men, disapproved of the death penalty. They considered that form of punishment out of date, immoral, and unsuitable for Christian states. In the opinion of some of them the death penalty ought to be replaced everywhere by imprisonment for life.

"I don't agree with you," said their host, the banker. "I have not tried either the death penalty or imprisonment for life, but if one may judge a priori, the death penalty is more moral and more humane than imprisonment for life. Capital punishment kills a man at once, but lifelong imprisonment kills him slowly. Which executioner is the more humane, he who kills you in a few minutes or he who drags the life out of you in the course of many years?"

"Both are equally immoral," observed one of the guests, "for they both have the same object—to take away life. The state is not God. It has not the right to take away what it cannot restore when it wants to."

Among the guests was a young lawyer, a young man of five-and-twenty. When he was asked his opinion, he said:

"The death sentence and the life sentence are equally immoral, but if I had to choose between the death penalty and imprisonment for life, I would certainly choose the second. To live anyhow is better than not at all."

A lively discussion arose. The banker, who was younger and more nervous in those days, was suddenly carried away by excitement; he struck the table with his fist and shouted at the young man:

"It's not true! I'll bet you two million you wouldn't stay in solitary confinement for five years."

"If you mean that in earnest," said the young man, "I'll take the bet, but I would stay not five but fifteen years."

"Fifteen? Done!" cried the banker. "Gentlemen, I stake two million!"

"Agreed! You stake your millions and I stake my freedom!" said the young man.

And this wild, senseless bet was carried out! The banker, spoiled and frivolous, with millions beyond his reckoning, was delighted at the bet. At supper he made fun of the young man, and said:

"Think better of it, young man, while there is still time. To me two million is a trifle, but you are losing three or four of the best years of your life. I say three or four, because you won't stay longer. Don't forget either, you unhappy man, that voluntary confinement is a great deal harder to bear than compulsory. The thought that you have the right to step out in liberty at any moment will poison your whole existence in prison. I am sorry for you."

And now the banker, walking to and fro, remembered all this, and asked himself: "What was the object of that bet? What is the good of that man's losing fifteen years of his life and my throwing away two million? Can it prove that the death penalty is better or worse than imprisonment for life? No, no. It was all nonsensical and meaningless. On my part it was the caprice of a pampered man, and on his part simple greed for money. . . ."

Then he remembered what followed that evening. It was decided that the young man should spend the years of his captivity under the strictest supervision in one of the lodges in the banker's garden. It was agreed that for fifteen years he should not be free to cross the threshold of the lodge, to see human beings, to hear the human voice, or to receive letters and newspapers. He was allowed to have a musical instrument and books, and was allowed to write letters, to drink wine, and to smoke. By the terms of the agreement, the only relations he could have with the outer world were by a little window made purposely for that object. He might have anything he wanted—books, music, wine, and so on—in any quantity he desired by writing an order, but could only receive them through the window. The agreement provided for every detail and every trifle that would make his imprisonment strictly solitary, and bound the young man to stay there *exactly* fifteen years, beginning from twelve o'clock of November 14, 1870, and ending at twelve o'clock of November 14, 1885. The slightest attempt on his part to break the conditions, if only two minutes before the end, released the banker from the obligation to pay him two million.

For the first year of his confinement, as far as one could judge from his brief notes, the prisoner suffered severely from loneliness and depression. The sounds of the piano could be heard continually day and night from his lodge. He refused wine and tobacco. Wine, he wrote, excites the desires, and desires are the worst foes of the prisoner; and besides, nothing could be more dreary than drinking good wine and seeing no one. And tobacco spoiled the air of his room. In the first year the books he sent for were principally of a light character; novels with a complicated love plot, sensational and fantastic stories, and so on.

In the second year the piano was silent in the lodge, and the prisoner asked only for the classics. In the fifth year music was audible again, and the prisoner asked for wine. Those who watched him through the window said that all that year he spent doing nothing but eating and drinking and lying on his bed, frequently yawning and angrily talking to himself. He did not read books. Sometimes at night he would sit down to write; he would spend hours writing, and in the morning tear up all that he had written. More than once he could be heard crying.

In the second half of the sixth year the prisoner began zealously studying languages, philosophy, and history. He threw himself eagerly into these studies—so much so that the banker had enough to do to get him the books he ordered. In the course of four years some six hundred volumes were procured at his request. It was during this period that the banker received the following letter from his prisoner:

"My dear Jailer, I write you these lines in six languages. Show them to people who know the languages. Let them read them. If they find not one mistake I implore you to fire a shot in the garden. That shot will show me that my efforts have not been thrown away. The geniuses of all ages and of all lands speak different languages, but the same flame burns in them all. Oh, if you only knew what unearthly happiness my soul feels now from being able to understand them!" The prisoner's desire was fulfilled. The banker ordered two shots to be fired in the garden.

Then after the tenth year, the prisoner sat immovably at the table and read nothing but the Gospel. It seemed strange to the banker that a man who in four years had mastered six hundred learned volumes should waste nearly a year over one thin book easy of comprehension. Theology and histories of religion followed the Gospels.

In the last two years of his confinement the prisoner read an immense quantity of books quite indiscriminately. At one time he was busy with the natural sciences, then he would ask for Byron or Shakespeare. There were notes in which he demanded at the same time books on chemistry, and a manual of medicine, and a novel, and some treatise on philosophy or theology. His reading suggested a man swimming in the sea among the wreckage of his ship, and trying to save his life by greedily clutching first at one spar and then at another.

2

The old banker remembered all of this, and thought:

"Tomorrow at twelve o'clock he will regain his freedom. By our agreement I ought to pay him two million. If I do pay him, it is all over with me: I shall be utterly ruined."

111

Fifteen years before, his millions had been beyond his reckoning; now he was afraid to ask himself which were greater, his debts or his assets. Desperate gambling on the stock exchange, wild speculation, and the excitability that he could not get over even in advancing years, had by degrees led to the decline of his fortune, and the proud, fearless, self-confident millionaire had become a banker of middling rank, trembling at every rise and fall in his investments. "Cursed bet!" muttered the old man, clutching his head in despair. "Why didn't the man die? He is only forty now. He will take my last penny from me, he will marry, will enjoy life, will gamble on the exchange; while I shall look at him with envy like a beggar, and hear from him every day the same sentence: 'I am indebted to you for the happiness of my life, let me help you!' No, it is too much! The one means of being saved from bankruptcy and disgrace is the death of that man!"

It struck three o'clock, the banker listened; everyone was asleep in the house, and nothing could be heard outside but the rustling of the chilled trees. Trying to make no noise, he took from a fireproof safe the key of the door that had not been opened for fifteen years, put on his overcoat, and went out of the house.

It was dark and cold in the garden. Rain was falling. A damp cutting wind was racing about the garden, howling and giving the trees no rest. The banker strained his eyes, but could see neither the earth nor the white statues, nor the lodge, nor the trees. Going to the spot where the lodge stood, he twice called the watchman. No answer followed. Evidently the watchman had sought shelter from the weather, and was now asleep somewhere either in the kitchen or in the greenhouse.

"If I had the pluck to carry out my intention," thought the old man, "suspicion would fall first upon the watchman."

He felt in the darkness for the steps and the door, and went into the entry of the lodge. Then he groped his way into a little passage and lighted a match. There was not a soul there. There was a bedstead with no bedding on it, and in the corner there was a dark cast-iron stove. The seals on the door leading to the prisoner's rooms were intact.

When the match went out the old man, trembling with emotion, peeped through the little window. A candle was burning dimly in the prisoner's room. He was sitting at the table. Nothing could be seen but his back, the hair on his head, and his hands. Open books were lying on the table, on the two easy chairs, and on the carpet near the table.

Five minutes passed and the prisoner did not once stir. Fifteen years' imprisonment had taught him to sit still. The banker tapped at the window with his finger, and the prisoner made no movement whatever in response. Then the banker cautiously broke the seals off the door and put the key in the keyhole. The rusty lock gave a grating sound and the door creaked. The banker expected to hear at once footsteps and a cry of astonishment, but three minutes passed and it was as quiet as ever in the room. He made up his mind to go in.

At the table a man unlike ordinary people was sitting motionless. He was a skeleton with the skin drawn tight over his bones, with long curls like a woman's, and a shaggy beard. His face was yellow with an earthy tint in it, his cheeks were hollow, his back long and narrow, and the hand on which his shaggy head was propped was so thin and delicate that it was dreadful to look at it. His hair was already streaked with silver, and seeing his emaciated, aged-looking face, no one would have believed that he was only forty. He was asleep. . . . In front of his bowed head there lay on the table a sheet of paper on which there was something written in fine handwriting.

"Poor creature!" thought the banker, "he is asleep and most likely dreaming of the millions. And I have only to take this half-dead man, throw him on the bed, stifle him a little with the pillow, and the most conscientious expert would find no sign of a violent death. But let us first read what he has written here. . . ."

The banker took the page from the table and read as follows:

"Tomorrow at twelve o'clock I regain my freedom and the right to associate with other men, but before I leave this room and see sunshine, I think it necessary to say a few words to you. With a clear conscience I tell you, as before God, who beholds me, that I despise freedom and life and health, and all that in your books is called the good things of the world.

"For fifteen years I have been intently studying earthly life. It is true I have not seen the earth nor men, but in your books I have drunk fragrant wine, I have sung songs, I have hunted stags and wild boars in the forests, have loved women. . . . Beauties as ethereal as clouds, created by the magic of your poets and geniuses, have visited me at night, and have whispered in my ears wonderful tales that have set my brain in a whirl. In your books I have climbed to the peaks of Elburz and Mont Blanc, and from there I have seen the sun rise and have watched it at evening flood the sky, the ocean, and the mountaintops with gold and crimson. I have watched from there the lightning flashing over my head and cleaving the storm clouds. I have seen green forests, fields, rivers, lakes, towns. I have heard the singing of the sirens, and the strains of the shepherds' pipes; I have touched the wings of comely devils who flew down to converse with me of God. . . . In your books I have flung myself into the bottomless pit, performed miracles, slain, burned towns, preached new religions, conquered whole kingdoms. . . .

"Your books have given me wisdom. All that the unresting thought of man has created in the ages is compressed into a small compass in my brain. I know that I am wiser than all of you.

"And I despise your books, I despise wisdom and the blessings of this world. It is all worthless, fleeting, illusory, and deceptive, like a mirage. You may be proud, wise, and fine, but death will wipe you off the face of the earth as though you were no more than mice burrowing under the floor, and your posterity, your history, your immortal geniuses will burn or freeze together with the earthly globe.

"You have lost your reason and taken the wrong path. You have taken lies for truth, and hideousness for beauty. You would marvel if, owing to strange events of some sorts, frogs and lizards suddenly grew on apple and orange trees instead of fruit, or if roses began to smell like a sweating horse; so I marvel at you who exchange heaven for earth. I don't want to understand you.

"To prove to you in action how I despise all that you live by, I renounce the two million of which I once dreamed as of paradise and that now I despise. To deprive myself of the right to the money I shall go out from here five hours before the time fixed, and so break the compact. . . ."

When the banker had read this he laid the page on the table, kissed the strange man on the head, and went out of the lodge, weeping. At no other time, even when he had lost heavily on the stock exchange, had he felt so great a contempt for himself. When he got home he lay on his bed, but his tears and emotion kept him for hours from sleeping.

Next morning the watchmen ran in with pale faces, and told him they had seen the man who lived in the lodge climb out of the window into the garden, go to the gate, and disappear. The banker went at once with the servants to the lodge and made sure of the flight of his prisoner. To avoid arousing unnecessary talk, he took from the table the writing in which the millions were renounced, and when he got home locked it up in the fireproof safe.

THE SECRET LION

Alberto Álvaro Ríos

I was twelve and in junior high school and something happened that we didn't have a name for, but it was there nonetheless like a lion, and roaring, roaring that way the biggest things do. Everything changed. Just that. Like the rug, the one that gets pulled—or better, like the tablecloth those magicians pull where the stuff on the table stays the same but the gasp! from the audience makes the staying-the-same part not matter. Like that.

What happened was there were teachers now, not just one teacher, teach-erz, and we felt personally abandoned somehow. When a person had all these teachers now, he didn't get taken care of the same way, even though six was more than one. Arithmetic went out the door when we walked in. And we saw girls now, but they weren't the same girls we used to know because we couldn't talk to them anymore, not the same way we used to, certainly not to Sandy, even though she was my neighbor, too. Not even to her. She just played the piano all the time. And there were words, oh there were words in junior

119

high school, and we wanted to know what they were, and how a person did them—that's what school was supposed to be for. Only, in junior high school, school wasn't school, everything was backward-like. If you went up to a teacher and said the word to try and find out what it meant you got in trouble for saying it. So we didn't. And we figured it must have been that way about other stuff, too, so we never said anything about anything—we weren't stupid.

But my friend Sergio and I, we solved junior high school. We would come home from school on the bus, put our books away, change shoes, and go across the highway to the arroyo. It was the one place we were not supposed to go. So we did. This was, after all, what junior high had at least shown us. It was our river, though, our personal Mississippi, our friend from long back, and it was full of stories and all the branch forts we had built in it when we were still the Vikings of America, with our own symbol, which we had carved everywhere, even in the sand, which let the water take it. That was good, we had decided; whoever was at the end of this river would know about us.

At the very very top of our growing lungs, what we would do down there was shout every dirty word we could think of, in every combination we could come up with, and we would yell about girls, and all the things we wanted to do with them, as loud as we could—we didn't know what we wanted to do with them, just things—and we would yell about teachers, and how we loved some of them, like Miss Crevelone, and how we wanted to dissect some of them, making signs of the cross, like priests, and we would yell this stuff over and over because it felt good, we couldn't explain why, it just felt good and for the first time in our lives there was nobody to tell us we couldn't. So we did.

One Thursday we were walking along shouting this way, and the railroad, the Southern Pacific, which ran above and along the far side of the arroyo, had dropped a grinding ball down there, which was, we found out later, a cannonball thing used in mining. A bunch of them were put in a big vat which turned around and crushed the ore. One had been dropped, or thrown—what do caboose men do when they get bored—but it got down there regardless and as we were walking along yelling about one girl or another, a particular Claudia, we found it, one of these things, looked at it, picked it up, and got very excited, and held it and passed it back and forth, and we were saying "Guythisis, this is, geeGuythis . . .": we had this perception about nature then, that nature is imperfect and that round things are perfect: we said "GuyGodthis is perfect, thisisthis is perfect, it's round, round and heavy, it'sit's the best thing we'veeverseen. Whatisit?" We didn't know. We just knew it was great. We just, whatever, we played with it, held it some more.

And then we had to decide what to do with it. We knew, because of a lot of things, that if we were going to take this and show it to anybody, this discovery, this best thing, was going to be taken away from us. That's the way it works with little kids, like all the polished quartz, the tons of it we had collected piece by piece over the years. Junior high kids too. If we took it home, my mother, we knew, was going to look at it and say "throw that dirty thing in the, get rid of it." Simple like, like that. "But Ma it's the best thing I" "Getridofit." Simple.

So we didn't. Take it home. Instead, we came up with the answer. We dug a hole and we buried it. And we marked it secretly. Lots of secret signs. And came back the next week to dig it up and, we didn't know, pass it around some more or something, but we didn't find it. We dug up that whole bank, and we never found it again. We tried.

Sergio and I talked about that ball or whatever it was when we couldn't find it. All we used were small words, neat, good. Kid words. What we were really saying, but didn't know the words, was how much that ball was like that place, that whole arroyo: couldn't tell anybody about it, didn't understand what it was, didn't have a name for it. It just felt good. It was just perfect in the way it was that place, that whole going to that place, that whole junior high school lion. It was just iron-heavy, it had no name, it felt good or not, we couldn't take it home to show our mothers, and once we buried it, it was gone forever.

The ball was gone, like the first reasons we had come to that arroyo years earlier, like the first time we had seen the arroyo, it was gone like everything else that had been taken away. This was not our first lesson. We stopped going to the arroyo after not finding the thing, the same way we had stopped going there years earlier and headed for the mountains. Nature seemed to keep pushing us around one way or another, teaching us the same thing every place we ended up. Nature's gang was tough that way, teaching us stuff.

When we were young we moved away from town, me and my family. Sergio's was already out there. Out in the wilds. Or at least the new place seemed like the wilds since everything looks bigger the smaller a man is. I was five, I guess, and we had moved three miles north of Nogales where we had lived, three miles north of the Mexican border. We looked across the highway in one direction and there was the arroyo; hills stood up in the other direction. Mountains, for a small man.

When the first summer came the very first place we went to was of course the one place we weren't supposed to go, the arroyo. We went down in there and found water running, summer rainwater mostly, and we went swimming. But every third or fourth or fifth day, the sewage treatment plant that was, we found out, upstream, would release whatever it was that it released, and we would never know exactly what day that was, and a person really couldn't tell right off by looking at the water, not every time, not so a person could get out in time. So, we went swimming that summer and some days we had a lot of fun. Some days we didn't. We found a thousand ways to explain what happened on those other days, constructing elaborate stories about the neighborhood dogs, and hadn't she, my mother, miscalculated her step before, too? But she knew something was up because we'd come running into the house those days, wanting to take a shower, even—if this can be imagined—in the middle of the day.

That was the first time we stopped going to the arroyo. It taught us to look the other way. We decided, as the second side of summer came, we wanted to go into the mountains. They were still mountains then. We went running in one summer Thursday morning, my friend Sergio and I, into my mother's kitchen, and said, well, what'zin, what'zin those hills over there—we used her word so she'd understand us—and she said nothingdon'tworryaboutit. So we went out, and we weren't dumb, we thought with our eyes to each other, ohhoshe'strying-tokeepsomethingfromus. We knew adults.

We had read the books, after all; we knew about bridges and castles and wildtreacherousraging alligatormouth rivers. We wanted them. So we were going to go out and get them. We went back that morning into that kitchen and we said "We're going out there, we're going into the hills, we're going away for three days, don't worry." She said, "All right."

"You know," I said to Sergio, "if we're going to go away for three days, well, we ought to at least pack a lunch."

But we were two young boys with no patience for what we thought at the time was mom-stuff: making sa-and-wiches. My mother didn't offer. So we got out little kid knapsacks that my mother had sewn for us, and into them we put the jar of mustard. A loaf of bread. Knivesforksplates, bottles of Coke, a can opener. This was lunch for the two of us. And we were weighed down, humped over to be strong enough to carry this stuff. But we started walking anyway, into the hills. We were going to eat berries and stuff otherwise. "Goodbye." My mom said that.

After the first hill we were dead. But we walked. My mother could still see us. And we kept walking. We walked until we got to where the sun is straight overhead, noon. That place. Where that is doesn't matter; it's time to eat. The truth is we weren't anywhere close to that place. We just agreed that the sun was overhead and that it was time to eat, and by tilting our heads a little we could make that the truth.

"We really ought to start looking for a place to eat."

"Yeah. Let's look for a good place to eat." We went back and forth saying that for fifteen minutes, making it lunch-time because that's what we always said back and forth before lunchtimes at home. "Yeah, I'm hungry all right." I nodded my head. "Yeah, I'm hungry all right too. I'm hungry." He nodded his head. I nodded my head back. After a good deal more nodding, we were ready, just as we came over a little hill. We hadn't found the mountains yet. This was a little hill.

And on the other side of this hill we found heaven.

It was just what we thought it would be.

Perfect. Heaven was green, like nothing else in Arizona. And it wasn't a cemetery or like that because we had seen cemeteries and they had gravestones and stuff and this didn't. This was perfect, had trees, lots of trees, had birds, like we had never seen before. It was like *The Wizard of Oz*, like when they got to

Oz and everything was so green, so emerald, they had to wear those glasses, and we ran just like them, laughing, laughing that way we did that moment, and we went running down to this clearing in it all, hitting each other that good way we did.

We got down there, we kept laughing, we kept hitting each other, we unpacked our stuff, and we started acting "rich." We knew all about how to do that, like blowing on our nails, then rubbing them on our chests for the shine. We made our sandwiches, opened our Cokes, got out the rest of the stuff, the salt and pepper shakers. I found this particular hole and I put my Coke right into it, a perfect fit, and I called it my Coke-holder. I got down next to it on my back, because everyone knows that rich people eat lying down, and I got my sandwich in one hand and put my other arm around the Coke in its holder. When I wanted a drink, I lifted my neck a little, put out my lips, and tipped my Coke a little with the crook of my elbow. Ah.

We were there, lying down, eating our sandwiches, laughing, throwing bread at each other and out for the birds. This was heaven. We were laughing and we couldn't believe it. My mother *was* keeping something from us, ah ha, but we had found her out. We even found water over at the side of the clearing to wash our plates with—we had brought plates. Sergio started washing his plates when he was done, and I was being rich with my Coke, and this day in summer was right.

When suddenly these two men came, from around a corner of trees and the tallest grass we had ever seen. They had bags on their backs, leather bags, bags and sticks.

We didn't know what clubs were, but I learned later, like I learned about the grinding balls. The two men yelled at us. Most specifically, one wanted me to take my Coke out of my Coke-holder so he could sink his golf ball into it.

Something got taken away from us that moment. Heaven. We grew up a little bit, and couldn't go backward. We learned. No one had ever told us about golf. They had told us about heaven. And it went away. We got golf in exchange.

We went back to the arroyo for the rest of that summer, and tried to have fun the best we could. We learned to be ready for finding the grinding ball. We loved it, and when we buried it we knew what would happen. The truth is, we didn't look so hard for it. We were two boys and twelve summers then, and not stupid. Things get taken away.

We buried it because it was perfect. We didn't tell my mother, but together it was all we talked about, till we forgot. It was the lion.

STAR FOOD

Ethan Canin

The summer I turned eighteen I disappointed both my parents for the first time. This hadn't happened before, since what disappointed one usually pleased the other. As a child, if I played broom hockey instead of going to school, my mother wept and my father took me outside later to find out how many goals I had scored. On the other hand, if I spent Saturday afternoon on the roof of my parents' grocery store staring up at the clouds instead of counting cracker cartons in the stockroom, my father took me to the back to talk about work and discipline, and my mother told me later to keep looking for things that no one else saw.

This was her theory. My mother felt that men like Leonardo da Vinci and Thomas Edison had simply stared long enough at regular objects until they saw new things, and thus my looking into the sky might someday make me a great man. She believed I had a worldly curiosity. My father believed I wanted to avoid stock work.

Stock work was an issue in our family, as were all the jobs that had to be done in a grocery store. Our store was called Star Food and above it an incandescent star revolved. Its circuits buzzed, and its yellow points, as thick as my knees, drooped with the slow melting of the bulb. On summer nights flying insects flocked in clouds around it, droves of them burning on the glass. One of my jobs was to go out on the roof, the sloping, eaved side that looked over the western half of Arcade, California, and clean them off the star. At night, when their black bodies stood out against the glass, when the wind carried in the marsh smell of the New Jerusalem River, I went into the attic, crawled out the dormer window onto the peaked roof, and slid across the shingles to where the pole rose like a lightning rod into the night. I reached with a wet rag and rubbed away the June bugs and pickerel moths until the star was yellow-white and steaming from the moisture. Then I turned and looked over Arcade, across the bright avenue and my dimly lighted high school in the distance, into the low hills where oak trees grew in rows on the curbs and where girls drove to school in their own convertibles. When my father came up on the roof sometimes to talk about the store, we fixed our eyes on the red tile roofs or the small clouds of blue barbecue smoke that floated above the hills on warm evenings. While the clean bulb buzzed and flickered behind us, we talked about loss leaders or keeping the elephant-ear plums stacked in neat triangles.

The summer I disappointed my parents, though, my father talked to me about a lot of other things. He also made me look in the other direction whenever we were on the roof together, not west to the hills and their clouds of barbecue smoke, but east toward the other part of town. We crawled up one slope of the roof, then down the other so I could see beyond the back alley where wash hung on lines in the moonlight, down to the neighborhoods across Route 5. These were the neighborhoods where men sat on the curbs on weekday afternoons, where rusted, wheel-less cars lay on blocks in the yards.

"*You're* going to end up on one of those curbs," my father told me.

Usually I stared farther into the clouds when he said something like that. He and my mother argued about what I did on the roof for so many hours at a time, and I hoped that by looking closely at the amazing borders of clouds I could confuse him. My mother believed I was on the verge of discovering something atmospheric, and I was sure she told my father this, so when he came upstairs, made me look across Route 5, and talked to me about how I was going to end up there, I squinted harder at the sky.

"You don't fool me for a second," he said.

He was up on the roof with me because I had been letting someone steal from the store.

From the time we first had the star on the roof, my mother believed her only son was destined for limited fame. Limited because she thought that true vision was distilled and could not be appreciated by everybody. I discovered this shortly after the star was installed, when I spent an hour looking out over the roofs and chimneys instead of helping my father stock a shipment of dairy. It was a hot day and the milk sat on the loading dock while he searched for me in the store and in our apartment next door. When he came up and found me, his neck was red and his footfalls shook the roof joists. At my age I was still allowed certain mistakes, but I'd seen the dairy truck arrive and knew I should have been downstairs, so it surprised me later, after I'd helped unload the milk, when my mother stopped beside me as I was sprinkling the leafy vegetables with a spray bottle.

"Dade, I don't want you to let anyone keep you from what you ought to be doing."

"I'm sorry," I said. "I should have helped with the milk earlier."

"No," she said, "that's not what I mean." Then she told me her theory of limited fame while I sprayed the cabbage and lettuce with the atomizer. It was the first time I had heard her idea. The world's most famous men, she said, presidents and emperors, generals and patriots, were men of vulgar fame, men who ruled the world because their ideas were obvious and could be understood by everybody. But there was also limited fame. Newton and Galileo and Enrico Fermi were men of limited fame, and as I stood there with the atomizer in my hands my mother's eyes watered over and she told me she knew in her heart that one day I was going to be a man of limited fame. I was twelve years old.

After that day I found I could avoid a certain amount of stock work by staying up on the roof and staring into the fine layers of stratus clouds that floated above Arcade. In the *Encyclopedia Americana* I read about cirrus and cumulus and thunderheads, about inversion layers and currents like the currents at sea, and in the afternoons I went upstairs and watched. The sky was a changing thing, I found out. It was more than a blue sheet. Twirling with pollen and sunlight, it began to transform itself.

Often as I stood on the roof my father came outside and swept the sidewalk across the street. Through the telephone poles and crossed power lines he looked up at me, his broom strokes small and fierce as if he were hoeing hard ground. It irked him that my mother encouraged me to stay on the roof.

He was a short man with direct habits and an understanding of how to get along in the world, and he believed that God rewarded only two things, courtesy and hard work. God did not reward looking at the sky. In the car my father acknowledged good drivers and in restaurants he left good tips. He knew the names of his customers. He never sold a rotten vegetable. He shook hands often, looked everyone in the eye, and on Friday nights when we went to the movies he made us sit in the front row of the theater. "Why should I pay to look over other people's shoulders?" he said. The movies made him talk. On the way back to the car he walked with his hands clasped behind him and greeted everyone who passed. He smiled. He mentioned the fineness of the evening as if he were the admiral or aviator we had just seen on the screen. "People like it," he said. "It's good for business." My mother was quiet, walking with her slender arms folded in front of her as if she were cold.

I liked the movies because I imagined myself doing everything the heroes did—deciding to invade at daybreak, swimming half the night against the seaward current—but whenever we left the theater I was disappointed. From the front row, life seemed like a clear set of decisions, but on the street afterward I realized that the world existed all around me and I didn't know what I wanted. The quiet of evening and the ordinariness of human voices startled me.

Sometimes on the roof, as I stared into the layers of horizon, the sounds on the street faded into this same ordinariness. One afternoon when I was standing under the star my father came outside and looked up to me. "You're in a trance," he called. I glanced down at him, then squinted back at the horizon. For a minute he waited, and then from across the street he threw a rock. He had a pitcher's arm and could have hit me if he wanted, but the rock sailed past me and clattered on the shingles. My mother came right out of the store anyway and stopped him. "I wanted him off the roof," I heard my father tell her later in the same frank voice in which he explained his position to vegetable salesmen. "If someone's throwing rocks at him he'll come down. He's no fool."

I was flattered by this, but my mother won the point and from then on I could stay up on the roof when I wanted. To appease my father I cleaned the electric star, and though he often came outside to sweep, he stopped telling me to come down. I thought about limited fame and spent a lot of time noticing the sky. When I looked closely it was a sea with waves and shifting colors, wind seams and denials of distance, and after a while I learned to look at it so that it entered my eye whole. It was blue liquid. I spent hours looking into its pale wash, looking for things, though I didn't know what. I looked for lines or sectors, the diamond shapes of daylight stars. Sometimes, silver-winged jets from the air force base across the hills turned the right way against the sun and went off like small flash bulbs on the horizon. There was nothing that struck me and stayed, though, nothing with the brilliance of white light or electric explosion that I thought came with discovery, so after a while I changed my idea of discovery. I just stood on the roof and stared. When my mother asked me, I told her that I might be seeing new things but that seeing change took time. "It's slow," I told her. "It may take years."

The first time I let her steal I chalked it up to surprise. I was working the front register when she walked in, a thin, tall woman in a plaid dress that looked wilted. She went right to the standup display of cut-price, nearly expired breads and crackers, where she took a loaf of rye from the shelf. Then she turned and looked me in the eye. We were looking into each

134

other's eyes when she walked out the front door. Through the blue and white LOOK UP TO STAR FOOD sign on the window I watched her cross the street.

There were two or three other shoppers in the store, and over the tops of the potato chip packages I could see my mother's broom. My father was in back unloading chicken parts. Nobody else had seen her come in; nobody had seen her leave. I locked the cash drawer and walked to the aisle where my mother was sweeping.

"I think someone just stole."

My mother wheeled a trash receptacle when she swept, and as I stood there she closed it, put down her broom, and wiped her face with her handkerchief. "You couldn't get him?"

"It was a her."

"A lady?"

"I couldn't chase her. She came in and took a loaf of rye and left."

I had chased plenty of shoplifters before. They were kids usually, in sneakers and coats too warm for the weather. I chased them up the aisle and out the door, then to the corner and around it while ahead of me they tried to toss whatever it was—Twinkies, freeze-pops—into the sidewalk hedges. They cried when I caught them, begged me not to tell their parents. First time, my father said, scare them real good. Second time, call the law. I took them back with me to the store, held them by the collar as we walked. Then I sat them in the straight-back chair in the stockroom and gave them a speech my father had written. It was printed on a blue index card taped to the door. DO YOU KNOW WHAT YOU HAVE DONE? it began. DO YOU KNOW WHAT IT IS TO STEAL? I learned to pause between the questions, pace the room, check the card. "Give them time to get scared," my father said. He was expert at this. He never talked to them until he had dusted the vegetables or run a couple of women through the register. "Why should I stop my work for a kid who steals from me?" he said. When he finally came into the stockroom he moved and spoke the way policemen do at the scene of an accident. His manner was slow and deliberate. First he asked me what they had stolen. If I had recovered whatever it was, he took it and held it up to the light, turned it over in his fingers as if it were of large value. Then he opened the freezer door and led the kid inside to talk about law and punishment amid the frozen beef carcasses. He paced as he spoke, breathed clouds of vapor into the air.

In the end, though, my mother usually got him to let them off. Once when he wouldn't, when he had called the police to pick up a third-offense boy who sat trembling in the stockroom, my mother called him to the front of the store to talk to a customer. In the stockroom we kept a key to the back door hidden under a silver samovar that belonged to my grandmother, and when my father was in front that afternoon my mother came to the rear, took it out, and opened the back door. She leaned down to the boy's ear. "Run," she said.

The next time she came in it happened the same way. My father was at the vegetable tier, stacking avocados. My mother was in back listening to the radio. It was afternoon. I rang in a customer, then looked up while I was putting the milk cartons in the bottom of the bag, and there she was. Her gray eyes were looking into mine. She had two cans of pineapple juice in her hands, and on the way out she held the door for an old woman.

That night I went up to clean the star. The air was clear. It was warm. When I finished wiping the glass I moved out over the edge of the eaves and looked into the distance where little turquoise squares—lighted swimming pools—stood out against the hills.

"Dade—"

It was my father's voice from behind the peak of the roof.

"Yes?"

"Come over to this side."

I mounted the shallow-pitched roof, went over the peak, and edged down the other slope to where I could see his silhouette against the lights on Route 5. He was smoking. I got up and we stood together at the edge of the shingled eaves. In front of us trucks rumbled by on the interstate, their trailers lit at the edges like the mast lights of ships.

"Look across the highway," he said.

"I am."

"What do you see?"

"Cars."

"What else?"

"Trucks."

For a while he didn't say anything. He dragged a few times on his cigarette, then pinched off the lit end and put the rest back in the pack. A couple of motorcycles went by, a car with one headlight, a bus.

"Do you know what it's like to live in a shack?" he said.

"No."

"You don't want to end up in a place like that. And it's damn easy to do if you don't know what you want. You know how easy it is?"

"Easy," I said.

"You have to know what you want."

For years my father had been trying to teach me competence and industry. Since I was nine I had been squeeze-drying mops before returning them to the closet, double-counting change, sweeping under the lip of the vegetable bins even if the dirt there was invisible to customers. On the basis of industry, my father said, Star Food had grown from a two-aisle, one-freezer corner store to the largest grocery in Arcade. When I was eight he had bought the failing gas station next door and built additions, so that now Star Food had nine aisles, separate coolers for dairy, soda, and beer, a tiered vegetable stand, a glass-fronted butcher counter, a part-time butcher, and, under what used to be the rain roof of the failing gas station, free parking while you shopped. When I started high school we moved into the apartment next door, and at meals we discussed store improvements. Soon my father invented a grid system for easy location of foods. He stayed up one night and painted, and the next morning there was a new coordinate system on the ceiling of the store. It was a grid, A through J, 1 through 10. For weeks there were drops of blue paint in his eyelashes.

A few days later my mother pasted up fluorescent stars among the grid squares. She knew about the real constellations and was accurate with the ones she stuck to the ceiling, even though she also knew that the aisle lights in Star Food stayed on day and night, so that her stars were going to be invisible. We saw them only once, in fact, in a blackout a few months later, when they lit up in hazy clusters around the store.

"Do you know why I did it?" she asked me the night of the blackout as we stood beneath their pale light.

"No."

"Because of the idea."

She was full of ideas, and one was that I was accomplishing something on the shallow-pitched section of our roof. Sometimes she sat at the dormer window and watched me. Through the glass I could see the slender outlines of her cheekbones. "What do you see?" she asked. On warm nights she leaned over the sill and pointed out the constellations. "They are the illumination of great minds," she said.

After the woman walked out the second time I began to think a lot about what I wanted. I tried to discover what it was, and I had an idea it would come to me on the roof. In the evenings I sat up there and thought. I looked for signs. I threw pebbles down into the street and watched where they hit. I read the newspaper, and stories about ballplayers or jazz musicians began to catch my eye. When he was ten years old, Johnny Unitas strung a tire from a tree limb and spent afternoons throwing a football through it as it swung. Dizzy Gillespie played with an orchestra when he was seven. There was an emperor who ruled China at age eight. What could be said about me? He swept the dirt no one could see under the lip of the vegetable bins.

The day after the woman had walked out the second time, my mother came up on the roof while I was cleaning the star. She usually wore medium heels and stayed away from the shingled roof, but that night she came up. I had been over the glass once when I saw her coming through the dormer window, skirt hem and white shoes lit by moonlight. Most of the insects were cleaned off and steam was drifting up into the night. She came through the window, took off her shoes, and edged down the roof until she was standing next to me at the star. "It's a beautiful night," she said.

"Cool."

"Dade, when you're up here do you ever think about what is in the mind of a great man when he makes a discovery?"

The night was just making its transition from the thin sky to the thick, the air was taking on weight, and at the horizon distances were shortening. I looked out over the plain and tried to think of an answer. That day I had been thinking about a story my father occasionally told. Just before he and my mother were married he took her to the top of the hills that surround Arcade. They stood with the New Jerusalem River, western California, and the sea on their left, and Arcade on their right. My father has always planned things well, and that day as they stood in the hill pass a thunderstorm covered everything west, while Arcade, shielded by hills, was lit by the sun. He asked her which way she wanted to go. She must have realized it was a test, because she thought for a moment and then looked to the right, and when they drove down from the hills that day my father mentioned the idea of a grocery. Star Food didn't open for a year after, but that was its conception, I think, in my father's mind. That afternoon as they stood with the New Jerusalem flowing below them, the plains before them, and my mother in a cotton skirt she had made herself, I think my father must have seen right through to the end of his life.

I had been trying to see right through the end of my life, too, but these thoughts never led me in any direction. Sometimes I sat and remembered the unusual things that had happened to me. Once I had found the perfect, shed skin of a rattlesnake. My mother told my father that this indicated my potential for science. I was on the roof another time when it hailed apricot-size balls of ice on a summer afternoon. The day was hot and there was only one cloud, but as it approached from the distance it spread a shaft of darkness below it as if it had fallen through itself to the earth, and when it reached the New Jerusalem the river began throwing up spouts of water. Then it crossed onto land and I could see the hailstones denting parked cars. I went back inside the attic and watched it pass, and when I came outside again and picked up the ice balls that rolled between the corrugated roof spouts, their prickly edges melted in my fingers. In a minute they were gone. That was the rarest thing that ever happened to me. Now I waited for rare things because it seemed to me that if you traced back the lives of men you arrived at some sort of sign, rainstorm at one horizon and sunlight at the other. On the roof I waited for mine. Sometimes I thought about the woman and sometimes I looked for silhouettes in the blue shapes between the clouds.

"Your father thinks you should be thinking about the store," said my mother.

"I know."

"You'll own the store some day."

There was a carpet of cirrus clouds in the distance, and we watched them as their bottom edges were gradually lit by the rising moon. My mother tilted back her head and looked up into the stars. "What beautiful names," she said. "Cassiopeia, Lyra, Aquila."

"The Big Dipper," I said.

"Dade?"

"Yes?"

"I saw the lady come in yesterday."

"I didn't chase her."

"I know."

"What do you think of that?"

"I think you're doing more important things," she said. "Dreams are more important than rye bread." She took the bobby pins from her hair and held them in her palm. "Dade, tell me the truth. What do you think about when you come up here?"

In the distance there were car lights, trees, aluminum power poles. There were several ways I could have answered.

I said, "I think I'm about to make a discovery."

———

After that my mother began meeting me at the bottom of the stairs when I came down from the roof. She smiled expectantly. I snapped my fingers, tapped my feet. I blinked and looked at my canvas shoe-tips. She kept smiling. I didn't like this so I tried not coming down for entire afternoons, but this only made her look more expectant. On the roof my thoughts piled into one another. I couldn't even think of something that was undiscovered. I stood and thought about the woman.

Then my mother began leaving little snacks on the sill of the dormer window. Crackers, cut apples, apricots. She arranged them in fan shapes or twirls on a plate, and after a few days I started working regular hours again. I wore my smock and checked customers through the register and went upstairs only in the evenings. I came down after my mother had gone to sleep. I was afraid the woman was coming back, but I couldn't face my mother twice a day at the bottom of the stairs. So I worked and looked up at the door whenever customers entered. I did stock work when I could, stayed in back where the air was refrigerated, but I sweated anyway. I unloaded melons, tuna fish, cereal. I counted the cases of freeze-pops, priced the cans of All-American ham. At the swinging door between the stockroom and the back of the store my heart went dizzy. The woman knew something about me.

In the evenings on the roof I tried to think what it was. I saw mysterious new clouds, odd combinations of cirrus and stratus. How did she root me into the linoleum floor with her gray stare? Above me on the roof the sky was simmering. It was blue gas. I knew she was coming back.

It was raining when she did. The door opened and I felt the wet breeze, and when I looked up she was standing with her back to me in front of the shelves of cheese and dairy, and this time I came out from the counter and stopped behind her. She smelled of the rain outside.

"Look," I whispered, "why are you doing this to me?"

She didn't turn around. I moved closer. I was gathering my words, thinking of the blue index card, when the idea of limited fame came into my head. I stopped. How did human beings understand each other across huge spaces except with the lowest of ideas? I have never understood what it is about rain that smells, but as I stood there behind the woman I suddenly realized I was smelling the inside of clouds. What was between us at that moment was an idea we had created ourselves. When she left with a carton of milk in her hand I couldn't speak.

On the roof that evening I looked into the sky, out over the plains, along the uneven horizon. I thought of the view my father had seen when he was a young man. I wondered whether he had imagined Star Food then. The sun was setting. The blues and oranges were mixing into black, and in the distance windows were lighting up along the hillsides.

"Tell me what I want," I said then. I moved closer to the edge of the eaves and repeated it. I looked down over the alley, into the kitchens across the way, into living rooms, bedrooms, across slate rooftops. "Tell me what I want," I called. Cars pulled in and out of the parking lot. Big rigs rushed by on the interstate. The air around me was as cool as water, the lighted swimming pools like pieces of the daytime sky. An important moment seemed to be rushing up. "Tell me what I want," I said again.

Then I heard my father open the window and come out onto the roof. He walked down and stood next to me, the bald spot on top of his head reflecting the streetlight. He took out a cigarette, smoked it for a while, pinched off the end. A bird fluttered around the light pole across the street. A car crossed below us with the words JUST MARRIED on the roof.

"Look," he said, "your mother's tried to make me understand this." He paused to put the unsmoked butt back in the pack. "And maybe I can. You think the gal's a little down and out; you don't want to kick her when she's down. OK, I can understand that. So I've decided something, and you want to know what?"

He shifted his hands in his pockets and took a few steps toward the edge of the roof.

"You want to know what?"

"What?"

"I'm taking you off the hook. Your mother says you've got a few thoughts, that maybe you're on the verge of something, so I decided it's OK if you let the lady go if she comes in again."

"What?"

"I said it's OK if you let the gal go. You don't have to chase her."

"You're going to let her steal?"

"No," he said. "I hired a guard."

He was there the next morning in clothes that were all dark blue. Pants, shirt, cap, socks. He was only two or three years older than I was. My father introduced him to me as Mr. Sellers. "Mr. Sellers," he said, "this is Dade." He had a badge on his chest and a ring of keys the size of a doughnut on his belt. At the door he sat jingling them.

I didn't say much to him, and when I did my father came out from the back and counted register receipts or stocked impulse items near where he sat. We weren't saying anything important, though. Mr. Sellers didn't carry a gun, only the doughnut-size key ring, so I asked him if he wished he did.

"Sure," he said.

"Would you use it?"

"If I had to."

I thought of him using his gun if he had to. His hands were thick and their backs were covered with hair. This seemed to go along with shooting somebody if he had to. My hands were thin and white and the hair on them was like the hair on a girl's cheek.

During the days he stayed by the front. He smiled at customers and held the door for them, and my father brought him sodas every hour or so. Whenever the guard smiled at a customer I thought of him trying to decide whether he was looking at the shoplifter.

And then one evening everything changed.

I was on the roof. The sun was low, throwing slanted light. From beyond the New Jerusalem and behind the hills, four air force jets appeared. They disappeared, then appeared again, silver dots trailing white tails. They climbed and cut and looped back, showing dark and light like a school of fish. When they turned against the sun their wings flashed. Between the hills and the river they dipped low onto the plain, then shot upward and toward me. One dipped, the others followed. Across the New Jerusalem they turned back and made two great circles, one inside the other, then dipped again and leveled off in my direction. The sky seemed small enough for them to fall through. I could see the double tails, then the wings and the jets. From across the river they shot straight toward the store, angling up so I could see the V-wings and camouflage and rounded bomb bays, and I covered my ears, and in a moment they were across the water and then they were above me, and as they passed over they barrel-rolled and flew upside down and showed me their black cockpit glass so that my heart came up into my mouth.

I stood there while they turned again behind me and lifted back toward the hills, trailing threads of vapor, and by the time their booms subsided I knew I wanted the woman to be caught. I had seen a sign. Suddenly the sky was water-clear. Distances moved in, houses stood out against the hills, and it seemed to me that I had turned a corner and now looked over a rain-washed street. The woman was a thief. This was a simple fact and it presented itself to me simply. I felt the world dictating its course.

I went downstairs and told my father I was ready to catch her. He looked at me, rolled the chewing gum in his cheek. "I'll be damned."

"My life is making sense," I said.

When I unloaded potato chips that night I laid the bags in the aluminum racks as if I were putting children to sleep in their beds. Dust had gathered under the lip of the vegetable bins, so I swept and mopped there and ran a wet cloth over the stalls. My father slapped me on the back a couple of times. In school once I had looked through a microscope at the tip of my own finger, and now as I looked around the store everything seemed to have been magnified in the same way. I saw cracks in the linoleum floor, speckles of color in the walls.

This kept up for a couple of days, and all the time I waited for the woman to come in. After a while it was more than just waiting; I looked forward to the day when she would return. In my eyes she would find nothing but resolve. How bright the store seemed to me then when I swept, how velvety the skins of the melons beneath the sprayer bottle. When I went up to the roof I scrubbed the star with the wet cloth and came back down. I didn't stare into the clouds and I didn't think about the woman except with the thought of catching her. I described her perfectly for the guard. Her gray eyes. Her plaid dress.

After I started working like this my mother began to go to the back room in the afternoons and listen to music. When I swept the rear I heard the melodies of operas. They came from behind the stockroom door while I waited for the woman to return, and when my mother came out she had a look about her of disappointment. Her skin was pale and smooth, as if the blood had run to deeper parts.

"Dade," she said one afternoon as I stacked tomatoes in a pyramid, "it's easy to lose your dreams."

"I'm just stacking tomatoes."

She went back to the register. I went back to stacking, and my father, who'd been patting me on the back, winking at me from behind the butcher counter, came over and helped me.

"I notice your mother's been talking to you."

"A little."

We finished the tomatoes and moved on to the lettuce.

"Look," he said, "it's better to do what you have to do, so I wouldn't spend your time worrying frontwards and backwards about everything. Your life's not so long as you think it's going to be."

We stood there rolling heads of butterball lettuce up the shallow incline of the display cart. Next to me he smelled like Aqua Velva.

"The lettuce is looking good," I said.

Then I went up to the front of the store. "I'm not sure what my dreams are," I said to my mother. "And I'm never going to discover anything. All I've ever done on the roof is look at the clouds."

Then the door opened and the woman came in. I was standing in front of the counter, hands in my pockets, my mother's eyes watering over, the guard looking out the window at a couple of girls, everything revolving around the point of calm that, in retrospect, precedes surprises. I'd been waiting for her for a week, and now she came in. I realized I never expected her. She stood looking at me, and for a few moments I looked back. Then she realized what I was up to. She turned around to leave, and when her back was to me I stepped over and grabbed her.

I've never liked fishing much, even though I used to go with my father, because the moment a fish jumps on my line a tree's length away in the water I feel as if I've suddenly lost something. I'm always disappointed and sad, but now as I held the woman beneath the shoulder I felt none of this disappointment. I felt strong and good. She was thin, and I could make out the bones and tendons in her arm. As I led her back toward the stockroom, through the bread aisle, then the potato chips that were puffed and stacked like a row of pillows, I heard my mother begin to weep behind the register. Then my father came up behind me. I didn't turn around, but I knew he was there and I knew the deliberately calm way he was walking. "I'll be back as soon as I dust the melons," he said.

I held the woman tightly under her arm but despite this she moved in a light way, and suddenly, as we paused before the stockroom door, I felt as if I were leading her onto the dance floor. This flushed me with remorse. Don't spend your whole life looking backwards and forwards, I said to myself. Know what you want. I pushed the door open and we went in. The room was dark. It smelled of my whole life. I turned on the light and sat her down in the straight-back chair, then crossed the room and stood against the door. I had spoken

148

to many children as they sat in this chair. I had frightened them, collected the candy they had tried to hide between the cushions, and presented it to my father when he came in. Now I looked at the blue card. DO YOU KNOW WHAT YOU HAVE DONE? it said. DO YOU KNOW WHAT IT IS TO STEAL? I tried to think of what to say to the woman. She sat trembling slightly. I approached the chair and stood in front of her. She looked up at me. Her hair was gray around the roots.

"Do you want to go out the back?" I said.

She stood up and I took the key from under the silver samovar. My father would be there in a moment, so after I let her out I took my coat from the hook and followed. The evening was misty. She crossed the lot, and I hurried and came up next to her. We walked fast and stayed behind cars, and when we had gone a distance I turned and looked back. The stockroom door was closed. On the roof the star cast a pale light that whitened the aluminum-sided eaves.

It seemed we would be capable of a great communication now, but as we walked I realized I didn't know what to say to her. We went down the street without talking. The traffic was light, evening was approaching, and as we passed below some trees the streetlights suddenly came on. This moment has always amazed me. I knew the woman had seen it too, but it is always a disappointment to mention a thing like this. The streets and buildings took on their night shapes. Still we didn't say anything to each other. We kept walking beneath the pale violet of the lamps, and after a few more blocks I just stopped at one corner. She went on, crossed the street, and I lost sight of her.

I stood there until the world had rotated fully into the night, and for a while I tried to make myself aware of the spinning of the earth. Then I walked back toward the store. When they slept that night, my mother would dream of discovery and my father would dream of low-grade crooks. When I thought of this and the woman I was sad. It seemed you could never really know another person. I felt alone in the world, in the way that makes me aware of sound and temperature, as if I had just left a movie theater and stepped into an alley where a light rain was falling, and the wind was cool, and, from somewhere, other people's voices could be heard.

A Visit of Charity

Eudora Welty

It was midmorning—a very cold, bright day. Holding a potted plant before her, a girl of fourteen jumped off the bus in front of the Old Ladies' Home, on the outskirts of town. She wore a red coat, and her straight yellow hair was hanging down loose from the pointed white cap all the little girls were wearing that year. She stopped for a moment beside one of the prickly dark shrubs with which the city had beautified the Home, and then proceeded slowly toward the building, which was of whitewashed brick and reflected the winter sunlight like a block of ice. As she walked vaguely up the steps she shifted the small pot from hand to hand; then she had to set it down and remove her mittens before she could open the heavy door.

"I'm a Campfire Girl. . . . I have to pay a visit to some old lady," she told the nurse at the desk. This was a woman in a white uniform who looked as if she were cold; she had close-cut hair which stood up on the very top of her head exactly like a sea wave. Marian, the little girl, did not tell her that this visit would give her a minimum of only three points in her score.

"Acquainted with any of our residents?" asked the nurse. She lifted one eyebrow and spoke like a man.

"With any old ladies? No—but—that is, any of them will do," Marian stammered. With her free hand she pushed her hair behind her ears, as she did when it was time to study Science.

The nurse shrugged and rose. "You have a nice *multiflora cineraria* there," she remarked as she walked ahead down the hall of closed doors to pick out an old lady.

There was loose, bulging linoleum on the floor. Marian felt as if she were walking on the waves, but the nurse paid no attention to it. There was a smell in the hall like the interior of a clock. Everything was silent until, behind one of the doors, an old lady of some kind cleared her throat like a sheep bleating. This decided the nurse. Stopping in her tracks, she first extended her arm, bent her elbow, and leaned forward from the hips—all to examine the watch strapped to her wrist; then she gave a loud double-rap on the door.

"There are two in each room," the nurse remarked over her shoulder.

"Two what?" asked Marian without thinking. The sound like a sheep's bleating almost made her turn around and run back.

One old woman was pulling the door open in short, gradual jerks, and when she saw the nurse a strange smile forced her old face dangerously awry. Marian, suddenly propelled by the strong, impatient arm of the nurse, saw next the side-face of another old woman, even older, who was lying flat in bed with a cap on and a counterpane drawn up to her chin.

"Visitor," said the nurse, and after one more shove she was off up the hall.

Marian stood tongue-tied; both hands held the potted plant. The old woman, still with that terrible, square smile (which was a smile of welcome) stamped on her bony face, was waiting. . . . Perhaps she said something. The old woman in bed said nothing at all, and she did not look around.

Suddenly Marian saw a hand, quick as a bird claw, reach up in the air and pluck the white cap off her head. At the same time, another claw to match drew her all the way into the room, and the next moment the door closed behind her.

"My, my, my," said the old lady at her side.

Marian stood enclosed by a bed, a washstand and a chair; the tiny room had altogether too much furniture. Everything smelled wet—even the bare floor. She held onto the back of the chair, which was wicker and felt soft and damp. Her heart beat more and more slowly, her hands got colder and colder, and she could not hear whether the old women were saying anything or not. She could not see them very clearly. How dark it was! The window shade was down, and the only door was shut. Marian looked at the ceiling. . . . It was like being caught in a robbers' cave, just before one was murdered.

"Did you come to be our little girl for a while?" the first robber asked.

Then something was snatched from Marian's hand—the little potted plant.

"Flowers!" screamed the old woman. She stood holding the pot in an undecided way. "Pretty flowers," she added.

Then the old woman in bed cleared her throat and spoke. "They are not pretty," she said, still without looking around, but very distinctly.

Marian suddenly pitched against the chair and sat down in it.

"Pretty flowers," the first old woman insisted. "Pretty— pretty . . ."

Marian wished she had the little pot back for just a moment— she had forgotten to look at the plant herself before giving it away. What did it look like?

"Stinkweeds," said the other old woman sharply. She had a bunchy white forehead and red eyes like a sheep. Now she turned them toward Marian. The fogginess seemed to rise in her throat again, and she bleated, "Who—are—you?"

To her surprise, Marian could not remember her name. "I'm a Campfire Girl," she said finally.

"Watch out for the germs," said the old woman like a sheep, not addressing anyone.

"One came out last month to see us," said the first old woman.

A sheep or a germ? wondered Marian dreamily, holding onto the chair.

"Did not!" cried the other old woman.

"Did so! Read to us out of the Bible, and we enjoyed it!" screamed the first.

"Who enjoyed it!" said the woman in bed. Her mouth was unexpectedly small and sorrowful, like a pet's.

"We enjoyed it," insisted the other. "You enjoyed it—I enjoyed it."

"We all enjoyed it," said Marian; without realizing that she had said a word.

The first old woman had just finished putting the potted plant high, high on the top of the wardrobe, where it could hardly be seen from below. Marian wondered how she had ever succeeded in placing it there, how she could ever have reached so high.

"You mustn't pay any attention to old Addie," she now said to the little girl. "She's ailing today."

"Will you shut your mouth?" said the woman in bed. "I am not."

"You're a story."

"I can't stay but a minute—really, I can't," said Marian suddenly. She looked down at the wet floor and thought that if she were sick in here they would have to let her go.

With much to-do the first old woman sat down in a rocking chair—still another piece of furniture!—and began to rock. With the fingers of one hand she touched a very dirty cameo pin on her chest. "What do you do at school?" she asked.

"I don't know . . ." said Marian. She tried to think but she could not.

"Oh, but the flowers are beautiful," the old woman whispered. She seemed to rock faster and faster; Marian did not see how anyone could rock so fast.

"Ugly," said the woman in bed.

"If we bring flowers—" Marian began, and then fell silent. She had almost said that if Campfire Girls brought flowers to the Old Ladies' Home, the visit would count one extra point, and if they took a Bible with them on the bus and read it to the old ladies, it counted double. But the old woman had not listened, anyway; she was rocking and watching the other one, who watched back from the bed.

"Poor Addie is ailing. She has to take medicine—see?" she said, pointing a horny finger at a row of bottles on the table, and rocking so high that her black comfort shoes lifted off the floor like a little child's.

"I am no more sick than you are," said the woman in bed.

"Oh, yes you are!"

"I just got more sense than you have, that's all," said the other old woman, nodding her head.

"That's only the contrary way she talks when *you all* come," said the first old lady with sudden intimacy. She stopped the rocker with a neat pat of her feet and leaned toward Marian.

Her hand reached over—it felt like a petunia leaf, clinging and just a little sticky.

"Will you hush! Will you hush!" cried the other one.

Marian leaned back rigidly in her chair.

"When I was a little girl like you, I went to school and all," said the old woman in the same intimate, menacing voice. "Not here—another town. . . ."

"Hush!" said the sick woman. "You never went to school. You never came and you never went. You never were anything—only here. You never were born! You don't know anything. Your head is empty, your heart and hands and your old black purse are all empty, even that little old box that you brought with you you brought empty—you showed it to me. And yet you talk, talk, talk, talk, talk all the time until I think I'm losing my mind! Who are you? You're a stranger—a perfect stranger! Don't you know you're a stranger? Is it possible that they have actually done a thing like this to anyone—sent them in a stranger to talk, and rock, and tell away her whole long rigmarole? Do they seriously suppose that I'll be able to keep it up, day in, day out, night in, night out, living in the same room with a terrible old woman—forever?"

Marian saw the old woman's eyes grow bright and turn toward her. This old woman was looking at her with despair and calculation in her face. Her small lips suddenly dropped apart, and exposed a half circle of false teeth with tan gums.

"Come here, I want to tell you something," she whispered. "Come here!"

Marian was trembling, and her heart nearly stopped beating altogether for a moment.

"Now, now, Addie," said the first old woman. "That's not polite. Do you know what's really the matter with old Addie

158

today?" She, too, looked at Marian; one of her eyelids drooped low.

"The matter?" the child repeated stupidly. "What's the matter with her?"

"Why, she's mad because it's her birthday!" said the first old woman, beginning to rock again and giving a little crow as though she had answered her own riddle.

"It is not, it is not!" screamed the old woman in bed. "It is not my birthday, no one knows when that is but myself, and will you please be quiet and say nothing more, or I'll go straight out of my mind!" She turned her eyes toward Marian again, and presently she said in the soft, foggy voice, "When the worst comes to the worst, I ring this bell, and the nurse comes." One of her hands was drawn out from under the patched counterpane—a thin little hand with enormous black freckles. With a finger which would not hold still she pointed to a little bell on the table among the bottles.

"How old are you?" Marian breathed. Now she could see the old woman in bed very closely and plainly, and very abruptly, from all sides, as in dreams. She wondered about her—she wondered for a moment as though there was nothing else in the world to wonder about. It was the first time such a thing had happened to Marian.

"I won't tell!"

The old face on the pillow, where Marian was bending over it, slowly gathered and collapsed. Soft whimpers came out of the small open mouth. It was a sheep that she sounded like—a little lamb. Marian's face drew very close, the yellow hair hung forward.

"She's crying!" She turned a bright, burning face up to the first old woman.

"That's Addie for you," the old woman said spitefully.

Marian jumped up and moved toward the door. For the second time, the claw almost touched her hair, but it was not quick enough. The little girl put her cap on.

"Well, it was a real visit," said the old woman, following Marian through the doorway and all the way out into the hall. Then from behind she suddenly clutched the child with her sharp little fingers. In an affected, high-pitched whine she cried, "Oh, little girl, have you a penny to spare for a poor old woman that's not got anything of her own? We don't have a thing in the world—not a penny for candy—not a thing! Little girl, just a nickel—a penny—"

Marian pulled violently against the old hands for a moment before she was free. Then she ran down the hall, without looking behind her and without looking at the nurse, who was reading *Field & Stream* at her desk. The nurse, after another triple motion to consult her wristwatch, asked automatically the question put to visitors in all institutions: "Won't you stay and have dinner with *us*?"

Marian never replied. She pushed the heavy door open into the cold air and ran down the steps.

Under the prickly shrub she stooped and quickly, without being seen, retrieved a red apple she had hidden there.

Her yellow hair under the white cap, her scarlet coat, her bare knees all flashed in the sunlight as she ran to meet the big bus rocketing through the street.

"Wait for me!" she shouted. As though at an imperial command, the bus ground to a stop.

She jumped on and took a big bite out of the apple.

THE DESTRUCTORS

Graham Greene

1

It was on the eve of August Bank Holiday that the latest recruit became the leader of the Wormsley Common Gang. No one was surprised except Mike, but Mike at the age of nine was surprised by everything. "If you don't shut your mouth," somebody once said to him, "you'll get a frog down it." After that Mike kept his teeth tightly clamped except when the surprise was too great.

The new recruit had been with the gang since the beginning of the summer holidays, and there were possibilities about his brooding silence that all recognized. He never wasted a word even to tell his name until that was required of him by the rules. When he said "Trevor" it was a statement of fact, not as it would have been with the others a statement of shame or defiance. Nor did anyone laugh except Mike, who, finding himself without support, and meeting the dark gaze of the newcomer, opened his mouth and was quiet again. There was every reason why T., as he was afterwards referred to, should have been an object of mockery—there was his name (and they substituted the initial because otherwise they had no excuse not to laugh at it), the fact that his father, a former architect and present clerk, had "come down in the world" and that his mother considered herself better than the neighbours. What but an odd quality of danger, of the unpredictable, established him in the gang without any ignoble ceremony of initiation?

The gang met every morning in an impromptu car park, the site of the last bomb of the first blitz. The leader, who was known as Blackie, claimed to have heard it fall, and no one was precise enough in his dates to point out that he would have been one year old and fast asleep on the down platform of Wormsley Common Underground Station. On one side of the car park leant the first occupied house, No. 3, of the shattered Northwood Terrace—literally leant, for it had suffered from the blast of the bomb and the side walls were supported on wooden struts. A smaller bomb and some incendiaries had fallen beyond, so that the house stuck up like a jagged tooth and carried on the further wall relics of its neighbour, a dado, the remains of a fireplace. T., whose words were almost confined to voting "Yes" or "No" to the plan of operations proposed each day by Blackie, once startled the whole gang by saying broodingly, "Wren built that house, Father says."

"Who's Wren?"

"The man who built St. Paul's."

"Who cares?" Blackie said. "It's only Old Misery's."

Old Misery—whose real name was Thomas—had once been a builder and decorator. He lived alone in the crippled house, doing for himself: once a week you could see him coming back across the common with bread and vegetables, and once as the boys played in the car park he put his head over the smashed wall of his garden and looked at them.

"Been to the lav," one of the boys said, for it was common knowledge that since the bombs fell something had gone wrong with the pipes of the house and Old Misery was too mean to spend money on the property. He could do the redecorating himself at cost price, but he had never learnt plumbing. The lav was a wooden shed at the bottom of the narrow garden with a star-shaped hole in the door: it had escaped the blast which had smashed the house next door and sucked out the window frames of No. 3.

The next time the gang became aware of Mr. Thomas was more surprising. Blackie, Mike, and a thin yellow boy, who for some reason was called by his surname Summers, met him on the common coming back from the market. Mr. Thomas stopped them. He said glumly, "You belong to the lot that play in the car park?"

Mike was about to answer when Blackie stopped him. As the leader he had responsibilities. "Suppose we are?" he said ambiguously.

"I got some chocolates," Mr. Thomas said. "Don't like 'em myself. Here you are. Not enough to go round, I don't suppose. There never is," he added with sombre conviction. He handed over three packets of Smarties.

The gang was puzzled and perturbed by this action and tried to explain it away. "Bet someone dropped them and he picked 'em up," somebody suggested.

"Pinched 'em and then got in a bleeding funk," another thought aloud.

"It's a bribe," Summers said. "He wants us to stop bouncing balls on his wall."

"We'll show him we don't take bribes," Blackie said, and they sacrificed the whole morning to the game of bouncing that only Mike was young enough to enjoy. There was no sign from Mr. Thomas.

Next day T. astonished them all. He was late at the rendezvous, and the voting for that day's exploit took place without him. At Blackie's suggestion the gang was to disperse in pairs, take buses at random, and see how many free rides could be snatched from unwary conductors (the operation was to be carried out in pairs to avoid cheating). They were drawing lots for their companions when T. arrived.

"Where you been, T.?" Blackie asked. "You can't vote now. You know the rules."

"I've been *there*," T. said. He looked at the ground, as though he had thoughts to hide.

"Where?"

"At Old Misery's." Mike's mouth opened and then hurriedly closed again with a click. He had remembered the frog.

"At Old Misery's?" Blackie said. There was nothing in the rules against it, but he had a sensation that T. was treading on dangerous ground. He asked hopefully, "Did you break in?"

"No. I rang the bell."

"And what did you say?"

"I said I wanted to see his house."

"What did he do?"

"He showed it me."

"Pinch anything?"

"No."

"What did you do it for then?"

The gang had gathered round: it was as though an impromptu court were about to form and try some case of deviation. T. said, "It's a beautiful house," and still watching the ground,

166

meeting no one's eyes, he licked his lips first one way, then the other.

"What do you mean, a beautiful house?" Blackie asked with scorn.

"It's got a staircase two hundred years old like a corkscrew. Nothing holds it up."

"What do you mean, nothing holds it up. Does it float?"

"It's to do with opposite forces, Old Misery said."

"What else?"

"There's panelling."

"Like in the Blue Boar?"

"Two hundred years old."

"Is Old Misery two hundred years old?"

Mike laughed suddenly and then was quiet again. The meeting was in a serious mood. For the first time since T. had strolled into the car park on the first day of the holidays, his position was in danger. It only needed a single use of his real name and the gang would be at his heels.

"What did you do it for?" Blackie asked. He was just, he had no jealousy, he was anxious to retain T. in the gang if he could. It was the word *beautiful* that worried him—that belonged to a class world that you could still see parodied at the Wormsley Common Empire by a man wearing a top hat and a monocle, with a haw-haw accent. He was tempted to say, "My dear Trevor, old chap," and unleash his hellhounds. "If you'd broken in," he said sadly—that indeed would have been an exploit worthy of the gang.

"This was better," T. said. "I found out things." He continued to stare at his feet, not meeting anybody's eye, as though he were absorbed in some dream he was unwilling—or ashamed—to share.

"What things?"

"Old Misery's going to be away all tomorrow and Bank Holiday."

Blackie said with relief, "You mean we could break in?"

"And pinch things?" somebody asked.

Blackie said, "Nobody's going to pinch things. Breaking in—that's good enough, isn't it? We don't want any court stuff."

"I don't want to pinch anything," T. said. "I've got a better idea."

"What is it?"

T. raised eyes as grey and disturbed as the drab August day. "We'll pull it down," he said. "We'll destroy it."

Blackie gave a single hoot of laughter and then, like Mike, fell quiet, daunted by the serious implacable gaze. "What'd the police be doing all the time?" he said.

"They'd never know. We'd do it from inside. I've found a way in." He said with a sort of intensity, "We'd be like worms, don't you see, in an apple. When we came out again there'd be nothing there, no staircase, no panels, nothing but just walls, and then we'd make the walls fall down—somehow."

"We'd go to jug," Blackie said.

"Who's to prove? And anyway we wouldn't have pinched anything." He added without the smallest flicker of glee, "There wouldn't be anything to pinch after we'd finished."

"I've never heard of going to prison for breaking things," Summers said.

"There wouldn't be time," Blackie said. "I've seen house-breakers at work."

"There are twelve of us," T. said. "We'd organize."

"None of us know how . . ."

"I know," T. said. He looked across at Blackie. "Have you got a better plan?"

168

"Today," Mike said tactlessly, "we're pinching free rides . . ."

"Free rides," T. said. "Kid stuff. You can stand down, Blackie, if you'd rather . . ."

"The gang's got to vote."

"Put it up then."

Blackie said uneasily, "It's proposed that tomorrow and Monday we destroy Old Misery's house."

"Here, here," said a fat boy called Joe.

"Who's in favour?"

T. said, "It's carried."

"How do we start?" Summers asked.

"He'll tell you," Blackie said. It was the end of his leadership. He went away to the back of the car park and began to kick a stone, dribbling it this way and that. There was only one old Morris in the park, for few cars were left there except lorries: without an attendant there was no safety. He took a flying kick at the car and scraped a little paint off the rear mudguard. Beyond, paying no more attention to him than to a stranger, the gang had gathered round T.; Blackie was dimly aware of the fickleness of favour. He thought of going home, of never returning, of letting them all discover the hollowness of T.'s leadership, but suppose after all what T. proposed was possible—nothing like it had ever been done before. The fame of the Wormsley Common car-park gang would surely reach around London. There would be headlines in the papers. Even the grown-up gangs who ran the betting at the all-in wrestling and the barrow boys would hear with respect of how Old Misery's house had been destroyed. Driven by the pure, simple, and altruistic ambition of fame for the gang, Blackie came back to where T. stood in the shadow of Old Misery's wall.

T. was giving his orders with decision: it was as though this plan had been with him all his life, pondered through the seasons, now in his fifteenth year crystallized with the pain of puberty. "You," he said to Mike, "bring some big nails, the biggest you can find, and a hammer. Anybody who can, better bring a hammer and a screwdriver. We'll need plenty of them. Chisels too. We can't have too many chisels. Can anybody bring a saw?"

"I can," Mike said.

"Not a child's saw," T. said. "A real saw."

Blackie realized he had raised his hand like any ordinary member of the gang.

"Right, you bring one, Blackie. But now there's a difficulty. We want a hacksaw."

"What's a hacksaw?" someone asked.

"You can get 'em at Woolworth's," Summers said.

The fat boy called Joe said gloomily, "I knew it would end in a collection."

"I'll get one myself," T. said. "I don't want your money. But I can't buy a sledgehammer."

Blackie said, "They are working on No. 15. I know where they'll leave their stuff for Bank Holiday."

"Then that's all," T. said. "We meet here at nine sharp."

"I've got to go to church," Mike said.

"Come over the wall and whistle. We'll let you in."

2

On Sunday morning all were punctual except Blackie, even Mike. Mike had a stroke of luck. His mother felt ill, his father was tired after Saturday night, and he was told to go to church alone with many warnings of what would happen if he strayed. Blackie had difficulty in smuggling out the saw, and then in finding the sledgehammer at the back of No. 15. He approached the house from a lane at the rear of the garden, for fear of the policeman's beat along the main road. The tired evergreens kept off a stormy sun: another wet Bank Holiday was being prepared over the Atlantic, beginning in swirls of dust under the trees. Blackie climbed the wall into Misery's garden.

There was no sign of anybody anywhere. The lav stood like a tomb in a neglected graveyard. The curtains were drawn. The house slept. Blackie lumbered nearer with the saw and the sledgehammer. Perhaps after all nobody had turned up: the plan had been a wild invention: they had woken wiser. But when he came close to the back door he could hear a confusion of sound hardly louder than a hive in swarm: a clickety-clack, a bang bang, a scraping, a creaking, a sudden painful crack. He thought: it's true, and whistled.

They opened the back door to him and he came in. He had at once the impression of organization, very different from the old happy-go-lucky ways under his leadership. For a while he wandered up and down stairs looking for T. Nobody addressed him: he had a sense of great urgency, and already he could begin to see the plan. The interior of the house was being carefully demolished without touching the outer walls. Summers with hammer and chisel was ripping out the skirting boards in the ground floor dining room: he had already smashed the panels of the door. In the same room Joe was heaving up the parquet blocks, exposing the soft wood floorboards over the cellar. Coils of wire came out of the damaged skirting and Mike sat happily on the floor clipping the wires.

On the curved stairs two of the gang were working hard with an inadequate child's saw on the banisters—when they saw Blackie's big saw they signalled for it wordlessly. When he next saw them a quarter of the banisters had been dropped into the hall. He found T. at last in the bathroom—he sat moodily in the least cared-for room in the house, listening to the sounds coming up from below.

"You've really done it," Blackie said with awe. "What's going to happen?"

"We've only just begun," T. said. He looked at the sledge-hammer and gave his instructions. "You stay here and break the bath and wash basin. Don't bother about the pipes. They come later."

Mike appeared at the door. "I've finished the wires, T.," he said.

"Good. You've just got to go wandering round now. The kitchen's in the basement. Smash all the china and glass and bottles you can lay hold of. Don't turn on the taps—we don't want a flood—yet. Then go into all the rooms and turn out drawers. If they are locked get one of the others to break them open. Tear up any papers you find and smash all the orna-ments. Better take a carving knife with you from the kitchen. The bedroom's opposite here. Open the pillows and tear up the sheets. That's enough for the moment. And you, Blackie, when you've finished in here crack the plaster in the passage up with your sledgehammer."

"What are you going to do?" Blackie asked.

"I'm looking for something special," T. said.

It was nearly lunchtime before Blackie had finished and went in search of T. Chaos had advanced. The kitchen was a shambles of broken glass and china. The dining room was stripped of parquet, the skirting was up, the door had been taken off its hinges, and the destroyers had moved up a floor. Streaks of light came in through the closed shutters where they worked with the seriousness of creators—and destruction after all is a form of creation. A kind of imagination had seen this house as it had now become.

Mike said, "I've got to go home for dinner."

"Who else?" T. asked, but all the others on one excuse or another had brought provisions with them.

They squatted in the ruins of the room and swapped unwanted sandwiches. Half an hour for lunch and they were at work again. By the time Mike returned they were on the top floor, and by six the superficial damage was completed. The doors were all off, all the skirtings raised, the furniture pillaged and ripped and smashed—no one could have slept in the house except on a bed of broken plaster. T. gave his orders—eight o'clock next morning—and to escape notice they climbed singly over the garden wall, into the car park. Only Blackie and T. were left: the light had nearly gone, and when they touched a switch, nothing worked—Mike had done his job thoroughly.

"Did you find anything special?" Blackie asked.

T. nodded. "Come over here," he said, "and look." Out of both pockets he drew bundles of pound notes. "Old Misery's savings," he said. "Mike ripped out the mattress, but he missed them."

"What are you going to do? Share them?"

"We aren't thieves," T. said. "Nobody's going to steal anything from this house. I kept these for you and me—a celebration." He knelt down on the floor and counted them out—there were seventy in all. "We'll burn them," he said, "one by one," and taking it in turns they held a note upwards and lit the top corner, so that the flame burnt slowly towards their fingers. The grey ash floated above them and fell on their heads like age. "I'd like to see Old Misery's face when we are through," T. said.

"You hate him a lot?" Blackie asked.

"Of course I don't hate him," T. said. "There'd be no fun if I hated him." The last burning note illuminated his brooding face. "All this hate and love," he said, "it's soft, it's hooey. There's only things, Blackie," and he looked round the room crowded with the unfamiliar shadows of half-things, broken things, former things. "I'll race you home, Blackie," he said.

3

Next morning the serious destruction started. Two were missing—Mike and another boy whose parents were off to Southend and Brighton in spite of the slow warm drops that had begun to fall and the rumble of thunder in the estuary like the first guns of the old blitz. "We've got to hurry," T. said.

Summers was restive. "Haven't we done enough?" he asked. "I've been given a bob for slot machines. This is like work."

"We've hardly started," T. said. "Why, there's all the floors left, and the stairs. We haven't taken out a single window. You voted like the others. We are going to *destroy* this house. There won't be anything left when we've finished."

They began again on the first floor picking up the top floorboards next the outer wall, leaving the joists exposed. Then they sawed through the joists and retreated into the hall, as what was left of the floor heeled and sank. They had learnt with practice, and the second floor collapsed more easily. By the evening an odd exhilaration seized them as they looked down the great hollow of the house. They ran risks and made mistakes: when they thought of the windows it was too late to reach them. "Cor," Joe said, and dropped a penny down into the dry rubble-filled well. It cracked and spun amongst the broken glass.

"Why did we start this?" Summers asked with astonishment; T. was already on the ground, digging at the rubble, clearing a space along the outer wall. "Turn on the taps," he said. "It's too dark for anyone to see now, and in the morning it won't matter." The water overtook them on the stairs and fell through the floorless rooms.

It was then they heard Mike's whistle at the back. "Something's wrong," Blackie said. They could hear his urgent breathing as they unlocked the door.

"The bogies?" Summers asked.

"Old Misery," Mike said. "He's on his way." He put his head between his knees and retched. "Ran all the way," he said with pride.

"But why?" T. said. "He told me . . ." He protested with the fury of the child he had never been, "It isn't fair."

"He was down at Southend," Mike said, "and he was on the train coming back. Said it was too cold and wet." He paused and gazed at the water. "My, you've had a storm here. Is the roof leaking?"

"How long will he be?"

"Five minutes. I gave Ma the slip and ran."

"We better clear," Summers said. "We've done enough, anyway."

"Oh no, we haven't. Anybody could do this—" "this" was the shattered hollowed house with nothing left but the walls. Yet walls could be preserved. Facades were valuable. They could build inside again more beautifully than before. This could again be a home. He said angrily, "We've got to finish. Don't move. Let me think."

"There's no time," a boy said.

"There's got to be a way," T. said. "We couldn't have got this far . . ."

"We've done a lot," Blackie said.

"No. No, we haven't. Somebody watch the front."

"We can't do any more."

"He may come in at the back."

"Watch the back too." T. began to plead. "Just give me a minute and I'll fix it. I swear I'll fix it." But his authority had gone with his ambiguity. He was only one of the gang. "Please," he said.

"Please," Summers mimicked him, and then suddenly struck home with the fatal name. "Run along home, Trevor."

T. stood with his back to the rubble like a boxer knocked groggy against the ropes. He had no words as his dreams shook and slid. Then Blackie acted before the gang had time to laugh, pushing Summers backward. "I'll watch the front, T.," he said, and cautiously he opened the shutters of the hall. The grey wet common stretched ahead, and the lamps gleamed in the puddles. "Someone's coming, T. No, it's not him. What's your plan, T.?"

"Tell Mike to go out to the lav and hide close beside it. When he hears me whistle he's got to count ten and start to shout."

"Shout what?"

"Oh, 'Help,' anything."

"You hear, Mike," Blackie said. He was the leader again. He took a quick look between the shutters. "He's coming, T."

"Quick, Mike. The lav. Stay here, Blackie, all of you, till I yell."

"Where are you going, T.?"

"Don't worry. I'll see to this. I said I would, didn't I?"

Old Misery came limping off the common. He had mud on his shoes and he stopped to scrape them on the pavement's edge. He didn't want to soil his house, which stood jagged and dark between the bomb sites, saved so narrowly, as he believed, from destruction. Even the fanlight had been left unbroken by the bomb's blast. Somewhere somebody whistled. Old Misery looked sharply round. He didn't trust whistles. A child was shouting: it seemed to come from his own garden. Then a boy ran into the road from the car park. "Mr. Thomas," he called, "Mr. Thomas."

"What is it?"

"I'm terribly sorry, Mr. Thomas. One of us got taken short, and we thought you wouldn't mind, and now he can't get out."

"What do you mean, boy?"

"He's got stuck in your lav."

"He'd no business . . . Haven't I seen you before?"

"You showed me your house."

"So I did. So I did. That doesn't give you the right to . . ."

"Do hurry, Mr. Thomas. He'll suffocate."

"Nonsense. He can't suffocate. Wait till I put my bag in."

"I'll carry your bag."

"Oh no, you don't. I carry my own."

"This way, Mr. Thomas."

"I can't get in the garden that way. I've got to go through the house."

"But you *can* get in the garden this way, Mr. Thomas. We often do."

"You often do?" He followed the boy with a scandalized fascination. "When? What right . . . ?"

"Do you see . . . ? The wall's low."

"I'm not going to climb walls into my own garden. It's absurd."

"This is how we do it. One foot here, one foot there, and over." The boy's face peered down, an arm shot out, and Mr. Thomas found his bag taken and deposited on the other side of the wall.

"Give me back my bag," Mr. Thomas said. From the loo a boy yelled and yelled. "I'll call the police."

"Your bag's all right, Mr. Thomas. Look. One foot there. On your right. Now just above. To your left." Mr. Thomas climbed over his own garden wall. "Here's your bag, Mr. Thomas."

"I'll have the wall built up," Mr. Thomas said, "I'll not have you boys coming over here, using my loo." He stumbled on the path, but the boy caught his elbow and supported him. "Thank you, thank you, my boy," he murmured automatically. Somebody shouted again through the dark. "I'm coming, I'm coming," Mr. Thomas called. He said to the boy beside him, "I'm not unreasonable. Been a boy myself. As long as things are done regular. I don't mind you playing round the place Saturday mornings. Sometimes I like company. Only it's got to be regular. One of you asks leave and I say yes. Sometimes I'll say no. Won't feel like it. And you come in at the front door and out at the back. No garden walls."

"Do get him out, Mr. Thomas."

"He won't come to any harm in my loo," Mr. Thomas said, stumbling slowly down the garden. "Oh, my rheumatics," he said. "Always get 'em on Bank Holiday. I've got to go careful. There's loose stones here. Give me your hand. Do you know what my horoscope said yesterday? 'Abstain from any dealings in first half of week. Danger of serious crash.' That might be on this path," Mr. Thomas said. "They speak in parables and double meanings." He paused at the door of the loo. "What's the matter in there?" he called. There was no reply.

"Perhaps he's fainted," the boy said.

"Not in my loo. Here, you, come out," Mr. Thomas said, and giving a great jerk at the door he nearly fell on his back when it swung easily open. A hand first supported him and then pushed him hard. His head hit the opposite wall and he sat heavily down. His bag hit his feet. A hand whipped the key out of the lock and the door slammed. "Let me out," he called, and heard the key turn in the lock. "A serious crash," he thought, and felt dithery and confused and old.

A voice spoke to him softly through the star-shaped hole in the door. "Don't worry, Mr. Thomas," it said, "we won't hurt you, not if you stay quiet."

Mr. Thomas put his head between his hands and pondered. He had noticed that there was only one lorry in the car park, and he felt certain that the driver would not come for it before the morning. Nobody could hear him from the road in front, and the lane at the back was seldom used. Anyone who passed there would be hurrying home and would not pause for what they would certainly take to be drunken cries. And if he did call "Help," who, on a lonely Bank Holiday evening, would have the courage to investigate? Mr. Thomas sat on the loo and pondered with the wisdom of age.

After a while it seemed to him that there were sounds in the silence—they were faint and came from the direction of his house. He stood up and peered through the ventilation hole—between the cracks in one of the shutters he saw a light, not the light of a lamp, but the wavering light that a candle might give. Then he thought he heard the sound of hammering and scraping and chipping. He thought of burglars—perhaps they had employed the boy as a scout, but why should burglars engage in what sounded more and more like a stealthy form of carpentry? Mr. Thomas let out an experimental yell, but nobody answered. The noise could not even have reached his enemies.

4

Mike had gone home to bed, but the rest stayed. The question of leadership no longer concerned the gang. With nails, chisels, screwdrivers, anything that was sharp and penetrating, they moved around the inner walls worrying at the mortar between the bricks. They started too high, and it was Blackie who hit on the damp course and realized the work could be halved if they weakened the joints immediately above. It was a long, tiring, unamusing job, but at last it was finished. The gutted house stood there balanced on a few inches of mortar between the damp course and the bricks.

There remained the most dangerous task of all, out in the open at the edge of the bomb site. Summers was sent to watch the road for passersby, and Mr. Thomas, sitting on the loo, heard clearly now the sound of sawing. It no longer came from his house, and that a little reassured him. He felt less concerned. Perhaps the other noises too had no significance.

A voice spoke to him through the hole. "Mr. Thomas."

"Let me out," Mr. Thomas said sternly.

"Here's a blanket," the voice said, and a long grey sausage was worked through the hole and fell in swathes over Mr. Thomas's head.

"There's nothing personal," the voice said. "We want you to be comfortable tonight."

"Tonight," Mr. Thomas repeated incredulously.

"Catch," the voice said. "Penny buns—we've buttered them, and sausage rolls. We don't want you to starve, Mr. Thomas."

Mr. Thomas pleaded desperately. "A joke's a joke, boy. Let me out and I won't say a thing. I've got rheumatics. I got to sleep comfortable."

"You wouldn't be comfortable, not in your house, you wouldn't. Not now."

"What do you mean, boy?" But the footsteps receded. There was only the silence of night: no sound of sawing. Mr. Thomas tried one more yell, but he was daunted and rebuked by the silence—a long way off an owl hooted and made away again on its muffled flight through the soundless world.

At seven next morning the driver came to fetch his lorry. He climbed into the seat and tried to start the engine. He was vaguely aware of a voice shouting, but it didn't concern him. At last the engine responded and he backed the lorry until it touched the great wooden shore that supported Mr. Thomas's house. That way he could drive right out and down the street without reversing. The lorry moved forward, was momentarily checked as though something were pulling it from behind, and then went on to the sound of a long rumbling crash. The driver was astonished to see bricks bouncing ahead of him, while stones hit the roof of his cab. He put on his brakes. When he climbed out the whole landscape had suddenly altered. There was no house beside the car park, only a hill of rubble. He went round and examined the back of his lorry for damage, and found a rope tied there that was still twisted at the other end round part of a wooden strut.

The driver again became aware of somebody shouting. It came from the wooden erection which was the nearest thing to a house in that desolation of broken brick. The driver climbed the smashed wall and unlocked the door. Mr. Thomas came out of the loo. He was wearing a grey blanket to which flakes of pastry adhered. He gave a sobbing cry. "My house," he said. "Where's my house?"

"Search me," the driver said. His eye lit on the remains of a bath and what had once been a dresser and he began to laugh. There wasn't anything left anywhere.

"How dare you laugh," Mr. Thomas said. "It was my house. My house."

"I'm sorry," the driver said, making heroic efforts, but when he remembered the sudden check to his lorry, the crash of bricks falling, he became convulsed again. One moment the house had stood there with such dignity between the bomb sites like a man in a top hat, and then, bang, crash, there wasn't anything left—not anything. He said, "I'm sorry. I can't help it, Mr. Thomas. There's nothing personal, but you got to admit it's funny."

READING NONFICTION

Some nonfiction texts, like autobiographies or accounts of historical events, can read like stories. Others, like instruction manuals and some textbooks, are written purely to give information. In the Great Books Roundtable program, you will be reading nonfiction texts that include both narrative (story) and informational parts and that also raise questions for discussion.

Below are some questions you can ask yourself to help you better understand a nonfiction selection and discover issues you want to discuss. Try asking yourself these questions after your first reading of the text. Then, after rereading, consider how your answers have changed.

The reading strategies on pages xxii–xxiii are also helpful when reading nonfiction.

SUGGESTED QUESTIONS FOR NONFICTION

- How would you describe the author's tone?
- To whom does the author seem to be speaking?
- What is the author's attitude toward his or her subject?
- What is the structure of the text—is it like a list, a story, a persuasive essay, or something else? What is the effect of putting it together this way?
- What is the author trying to make you think, feel, or believe?
- Is the author asking you to take some kind of action?

How It Feels to Be Colored Me

Zora Neale Hurston

I am colored but I offer nothing in the way of extenuating circumstances except the fact that I am the only Negro in the United States whose grandfather on the mother's side was *not* an Indian chief.

I remember the very day that I became colored. Up to my thirteenth year I lived in the little Negro town of Eatonville, Florida. It is exclusively a colored town. The only white people I knew passed through the town going to or coming from Orlando. The native whites rode dusty horses, the Northern tourists chugged down the sandy village road in automobiles. The town knew the Southerners and never stopped cane chewing when they passed. But the Northerners were something else again. They were peered at cautiously from behind curtains by the timid. The more venturesome would come out on the porch to watch them go past and got just as much pleasure out of the tourists as the tourists got out of the village.

The front porch might seem a daring place for the rest of the town, but it was a gallery seat for me. My favorite place was atop the gatepost. Proscenium box for a born first-nighter. Not only did I enjoy the show, but I didn't mind the actors knowing that I liked it. I usually spoke to them in passing. I'd wave at them and when they returned my salute, I would say something like this: "Howdy-do-well-I-thank-you-where-you goin'?" Usually automobile or the horse paused at this, and after a queer exchange of compliments, I would probably "go a piece of the way" with them, as we say in farthest Florida. If one of my family happened to come to the front in time to see me, of course negotiations would be rudely broken off. But even so, it is clear that I was the first "welcome-to-our-state" Floridian, and I hope the Miami Chamber of Commerce will please take notice.

During this period, white people differed from colored to me only in that they rode through town and never lived there. They liked to hear me "speak pieces" and sing and wanted to see me dance the parse-me-la, and gave me generously of their small silver for doing these things, which seemed strange to me for I wanted to do them so much that I needed bribing to stop. Only they didn't know it. The colored people gave no dimes. They deplored any joyful tendencies in me, but I was their Zora nevertheless. I belonged to them, to the nearby hotels, to the county—everybody's Zora.

But changes came in the family when I was thirteen, and I was sent to school in Jacksonville. I left Eatonville, the town of the oleanders, as Zora. When I disembarked from the riverboat at Jacksonville, she was no more. It seemed that I had suffered a sea change. I was not Zora of Orange County any more, I was now a little colored girl. I found it out in certain ways.

In my heart as well as in the mirror, I became a fast brown—warranted not to rub nor run.

But I am not tragically colored. There is no great sorrow dammed up in my soul, nor lurking behind my eyes. I do not mind at all. I do not belong to the sobbing school of Negrohood who hold that nature somehow has given them a lowdown dirty deal and whose feelings are all hurt about it. Even in the helter-skelter skirmish that is my life, I have seen that the world is to the strong regardless of a little pigmentation more or less. No, I do not weep at the world—I am too busy sharpening my oyster knife.

Someone is always at my elbow reminding me that I am the granddaughter of slaves. It fails to register depression with me. Slavery is sixty years in the past. The operation was successful and the patient is doing well, thank you. The terrible struggle that made me an American out of a potential slave said "On the line!" The Reconstruction said "Get set!"; and the generation before said "Go!" I am off to a flying start and I must not halt in the stretch to look behind and weep. Slavery is the price I paid for civilization, and the choice was not with me. It is a bully adventure and worth all that I have paid through my ancestors for it. No one on earth ever had a greater chance for glory. The world to be won and nothing to be lost. It is thrilling to think—to know that for any act of mine, I shall get twice as much praise or twice as much blame. It is quite exciting to hold the center of the national stage, with the spectators not knowing whether to laugh or to weep.

The position of my white neighbor is much more difficult. No brown specter pulls up a chair beside me when I sit down to eat. No dark ghost thrusts its leg against mine in bed. The game of keeping what one has is never so exciting as the game of getting.

I do not always feel colored. Even now I often achieve the unconscious Zora of Eatonville before the Hegira. I feel most colored when I am thrown against a sharp white background.

For instance at Barnard. "Beside the waters of the Hudson" * I feel my race. Among the thousand white persons, I am a dark rock surged upon, and overswept, but through it all, I remain myself. When covered by the waters, I am; and the ebb but reveals me again.

Sometimes it is the other way around. A white person is set down in our midst, but the contrast is just as sharp for me. For instance, when I sit in the drafty basement that is the New World Cabaret with a white person, my color comes. We enter chatting about any little nothing that we have in common and are seated by the jazz waiters. In the abrupt way that jazz orchestras have, this one plunges into a number. It loses no time in circumlocutions, but gets right down to business. It constricts the thorax and splits the heart with its tempo and narcotic harmonies. This orchestra grows rambunctious, rears on its hind legs and attacks the tonal veil with primitive fury, rending it, clawing it until it breaks through to the jungle beyond. I follow those heathen—follow them exultingly. I dance wildly inside myself; I yell within, I whoop; I shake my assegai above my head, I hurl it true to the mark *yeeeeooww*! I am in the jungle and living in the jungle way. My face is painted red and yellow and my body is painted blue. My pulse is throbbing like a war drum. I want to slaughter something—

---

* A song commonly sung by seniors at Barnard College, where Hurston earned her university degree.

give pain, give death to what, I do not know. But the piece ends. The men of the orchestra wipe their lips and rest their fingers. I creep back slowly to the veneer we call civilization with the last tone and find the white friend sitting motionless in his seat, smoking calmly.

"Good music they have here," he remarks, drumming the table with his fingertips.

Music. The great blobs of purple and red emotion have not touched him. He has only heard what I felt. He is far away and I see him but dimly across the ocean and the continent that have fallen between us. He is so pale with his whiteness then and I am *so* colored.

At certain times I have no race, I am *me*. When I set my hat at a certain angle and saunter down Seventh Avenue, Harlem City, feeling as snooty as the lions in front of the Forty-Second Street Library, for instance. So far as my feelings are concerned, Peggy Hopkins Joyce on the Boule Mich with her gorgeous raiment, stately carriage, knees knocking together in a most aristocratic manner, has nothing on me. The cosmic Zora emerges. I belong to no race nor time. I am the eternal feminine with its string of beads.

I have no separate feeling about being an American citizen and colored. I am merely a fragment of the Great Soul that surges within the boundaries. My country, right or wrong.

Sometimes, I feel discriminated against, but it does not make me angry. It merely astonishes me. How *can* any deny themselves the pleasure of my company? It's beyond me.

But in the main, I feel like a brown bag of miscellany propped against a wall. Against a wall in company with other bags, white, red, and yellow. Pour out the contents, and there is discovered a jumble of small things priceless and worthless.

A first-water diamond, an empty spool, bits of broken glass, lengths of string, a key to a door long since crumbled away, a rusty knife blade, old shoes saved for a road that never was and never will be, a nail bent under the weight of things too heavy for any nail, a dried flower or two still a little fragrant. In your hand is the brown bag. On the ground before you is the jumble it held—so much like the jumble in the bags, could they be emptied, that all might be dumped in a single heap and the bags refilled without altering the content of any greatly. A bit of colored glass more or less would not matter. Perhaps that is how the Great Stuffer of Bags filled them in the first place—who knows?

I HAVE A DREAM

Martin Luther King Jr.

I am happy to join with you today in what will go down in history as the greatest demonstration for freedom in the history of our nation.

Five score years ago, a great American, in whose symbolic shadow we stand today, signed the Emancipation Proclamation. This momentous decree came as a great beacon light of hope to millions of Negro slaves who had been seared in the flames of withering injustice. It came as a joyous daybreak to end the long night of their captivity.

But one hundred years later, the Negro still is not free; one hundred years later, the life of the Negro is still sadly crippled by the manacles of segregation and the chains of discrimination; one hundred years later, the Negro lives on a lonely island of poverty in the midst of a vast ocean of material prosperity; one hundred years later, the Negro is still languished in the corners of American society and finds himself in exile in his own land.

So we've come here today to dramatize a shameful condition. In a sense we've come to our nation's capital to cash a check. When the architects of our republic wrote the magnificent words of the Constitution and the Declaration of Independence, they were signing a promissory note to which every American was to fall heir. This note was the promise that all men, yes, black men as well as white men, would be guaranteed the unalienable rights of life, liberty, and the pursuit of happiness.

It is obvious today that America has defaulted on this promissory note insofar as her citizens of color are concerned. Instead of honoring this sacred obligation, America has given the Negro people a bad check; a check which has come back marked "insufficient funds." But we refuse to believe that the bank of justice is bankrupt. We refuse to believe that there are insufficient funds in the great vaults of opportunity of this nation. And so we've come to cash this check, a check that will give us upon demand the riches of freedom and the security of justice.

We have also come to this hallowed spot to remind America of the fierce urgency of now. This is no time to engage in the luxury of cooling off or to take the tranquilizing drug of gradualism. Now is the time to make real the promises of democracy; now is the time to rise from the dark and desolate valley of segregation to the sunlit path of racial justice; now is the time to lift our nation from the quicksands of racial injustice to the solid rock of brotherhood; now is the time to make justice a reality for all of God's children. It would be fatal for the nation to overlook the urgency of the moment. This sweltering summer of the Negro's legitimate discontent will not pass until there is an invigorating autumn of freedom and equality.

Nineteen sixty-three is not an end, but a beginning. And those who hope that the Negro needed to blow off steam and will now be content, will have a rude awakening if the nation returns to business as usual. There will be neither rest nor tranquility in America until the Negro is granted his citizenship rights. The whirlwinds of revolt will continue to shake the foundations of our nation until the bright day of justice emerges.

But there is something that I must say to my people, who stand on the worn threshold which leads into the palace of justice. In the process of gaining our rightful place, we must not be guilty of wrongful deeds. Let us not seek to satisfy our thirst for freedom by drinking from the cup of bitterness and hatred. We must forever conduct our struggle on the high plain of dignity and discipline. We must not allow our creative protests to degenerate into physical violence. Again and again we must rise to the majestic heights of meeting physical force with soul force. The marvelous new militancy, which has engulfed the Negro community, must not lead us to a distrust of all white people. For many of our white brothers, as evidenced by their presence here today, have come to realize that their destiny is tied up with our destiny. And they have come to realize that their freedom is inextricably bound to our freedom. We cannot walk alone. And as we walk, we must make the pledge that we shall always march ahead. We cannot turn back.

There are those who are asking the devotees of civil rights, "When will you be satisfied?" We can never be satisfied as long as the Negro is the victim of the unspeakable horrors of police brutality; we can never be satisfied as long as our bodies, heavy with the fatigue of travel, cannot gain lodging in the motels of the highways and the hotels of the cities; we cannot be satisfied as long as the Negro's basic mobility is from a smaller ghetto to a larger one; we can never be satisfied as long as our children are stripped of their selfhood and robbed of their dignity by signs stating "For White Only"; we cannot be satisfied as long as the Negro in Mississippi cannot vote and a Negro in New York believes he has nothing for which to vote. No! No, we are not satisfied, and we will not be satisfied until "justice rolls down like waters and righteousness like a mighty stream." *

I am not unmindful that some of you have come here out of great trials and tribulations. Some of you have come fresh from narrow jail cells. Some of you have come from areas where your quest for freedom left you battered by the storms of persecution and staggered by the winds of police brutality. You have been the veterans of creative suffering. Continue to work with the faith that unearned suffering is redemptive. Go back to Mississippi. Go back to Alabama. Go back to South Carolina. Go back to Georgia. Go back to Louisiana. Go back to the slums and ghettos of our Northern cities, knowing that somehow this situation can and will be changed. Let us not wallow in the valley of despair.

I say to you today, my friends, so even though we face the difficulties of today and tomorrow, I still have a dream. It is a dream deeply rooted in the American dream. I have a dream that one day this nation will rise up and live out the true meaning of its creed, "We hold these truths to be self-evident, that all men are created equal." I have a dream that one day on the red hills of Georgia, sons of former slaves and the sons of former slave owners will be able to sit down together at the table of brotherhood. I have a dream that one day even the

---

* Quoted verse from the Bible (Amos 5:24).

state of Mississippi, a state sweltering with the heat of injustice, sweltering with the heat of oppression, will be transformed into an oasis of freedom and justice. I have a dream that my four little children will one day live in a nation where they will not be judged by the color of their skin, but by the content of their character.

I HAVE A DREAM TODAY!

I have a dream that one day down in Alabama—with its vicious racists, with its Governor having his lips dripping with the words of interposition and nullification—one day right there in Alabama, little black boys and black girls will be able to join hands with little white boys and white girls as sisters and brothers.

I HAVE A DREAM TODAY!

I have a dream that one day every valley shall be exalted, every hill and mountain shall be made low. The rough places will be plain and the crooked places will be made straight, "and the glory of the Lord shall be revealed, and all flesh shall see it together." *

This is our hope. This is the faith that I go back to the South with. With this faith we will be able to hew out of the mountain of despair, a stone of hope. With this faith we will be able to transform the jangling discords of our nation into a beautiful symphony of brotherhood. With this faith we will be able to work together, to pray together, to struggle together, to go to jail together, to stand up for freedom together, knowing that we will be free one day. And this will be the day. This will be the day when all of God's children will be able to sing with new meaning, "My country 'tis of thee, sweet land of liberty,

---

* A reference to a passage from the Bible (Isaiah 40:4).

of thee I sing. Land where my father died, land of the pilgrim's pride, from every mountainside, let freedom ring." And if America is to be a great nation, this must become true.

So let freedom ring from the prodigious hilltops of New Hampshire; let freedom ring from the mighty mountains of New York; let freedom ring from the heightening Alleghenies of Pennsylvania; let freedom ring from the snowcapped Rockies of Colorado; let freedom ring from the curvaceous slopes of California. But not only that. Let freedom ring from Stone Mountain of Georgia; let freedom ring from Lookout Mountain of Tennessee; let freedom ring from every hill and molehill of Mississippi. "From every mountainside, let freedom ring."

And when this happens, and when we allow freedom to ring, when we let it ring from every village and every hamlet, from every state and every city, we will be able to speed up that day when all of God's children, black men and white men, Jews and Gentiles, Protestants and Catholics, will be able to join hands and sing in the words of the old Negro spiritual: "Free at last. Free at last. Thank God Almighty, we are free at last."

READING POETRY

If you are puzzled about what to make of a poem, you are not alone. Poems are meant to be read over and over and discovered slowly. Asking questions about a poem can help you uncover more of its meaning and think about it in new ways.

Below are some questions you can ask yourself to help you better understand a poem and discover issues you want to discuss. Try asking yourself these questions after you read the poem once or twice. Then, after a couple more readings, consider how your answers have changed.

SUGGESTED QUESTIONS FOR POETRY

About the Poem and the Audience
- Who is the poem's speaker?
- What situation or event is happening?
- Who or what is the audience?
- How does the title relate to the rest of the poem?
- Does the poem have to do with a particular moment in history?
- Does the poem have to do with a particular culture or society?

About Poetic Language and Form

- What kind of form does the poem have? How does it look on the page?

- Does the poem use words in an unusual way?

- Is the way the words sound (not just what they mean) an important element of the poem?

- Does the poem use images to make the reader feel a certain way?

- What is the tone? How do you know?

WAYS TO READ POETRY

Below are some ways to read and mark a poem that can help you further explore the author's choice of rhythm, language, and structure.

Recognize Rhythm

- With a partner, take turns reading the poem aloud several times. Experiment with each reading by exaggerating the syllables of words, speeding up or slowing down your reading, or clapping out the poem's rhythm while you read.

- Read the poem as a whole class, clapping, stomping, or walking in time to the poem's rhythm as you read.

Listen to Language

- With a partner, take turns reading the poem aloud several times. Experiment with each reading by exaggerating your mouth movements, stressing the consonants or vowels of certain words, or communicating with your voice how certain words make you feel.

- Underline some of the poem's repeated sounds or letters. Reread the poem aloud, stressing the repetitions you underlined.

See the Structure

- Trace the end of each line of the poem with a pencil (as if connecting dots) to see what pattern the poem makes on the page.
- Read the poem aloud, taking a breath or pausing at the end of each *sentence* in the poem—wherever there is a period, question mark, or exclamation point. Then read the poem again, taking a breath or pausing at each *line break*—wherever the author stops a line. Compare the two readings. How were they different? How did each one make you feel about the poem? Did you notice anything new in either reading?

THE HAND

Mary Ruefle

The teacher asks a question.
You know the answer, you suspect
you are the only one in the classroom
who knows the answer, because the person
in question is yourself, and on that
you are the greatest living authority,
but you don't raise your hand.
You raise the top of your desk
and take out an apple.
You look out the window.
You don't raise your hand and there is
some essential beauty in your fingers,
which aren't even drumming, but lie
flat and peaceful.
The teacher repeats the question.
Outside the window, on an overhanging branch,
a robin is ruffling its feathers
and spring is in the air.

THE SONG OF WANDERING AENGUS

William Butler Yeats

I went out to the hazel wood,
Because a fire was in my head,
And cut and peeled a hazel wand,
And hooked a berry to a thread;
And when white moths were on the wing,
And moth-like stars were flickering out,
I dropped the berry in a stream
And caught a little silver trout.

When I had laid it on the floor
I went to blow the fire a-flame,
But something rustled on the floor,
And someone called me by my name:
It had become a glimmering girl
With apple blossom in her hair
Who called me by my name and ran
And faded through the brightening air.

Though I am old with wandering
Through hollow lands and hilly lands,
I will find out where she has gone,
And kiss her lips and take her hands;
And walk among long dappled grass,
And pluck till time and times are done
The silver apples of the moon,
The golden apples of the sun.

CHILD ON TOP OF A GREENHOUSE

Theodore Roethke

The wind billowing out the seat of my britches,
My feet crackling splinters of glass and dried putty,
The half-grown chrysanthemums staring up like accusers,
Up through the streaked glass, flashing with sunlight,
A few white clouds all rushing eastward,
A line of elms plunging and tossing like horses,
And everyone, everyone pointing up and shouting!

THE PARAKEETS

Alberto Blanco

They talk all day
and when it starts to get dark
they lower their voices
to converse with their own shadows
and with the silence.

They are like everybody,
the parakeets:
all day chatter
and at night bad dreams.

With their gold rings
on their clever faces,
brilliant feathers
and the heart restless
with speech.

They are like everybody,
the parakeets:
the ones that talk best
have separate cages.

MENDING WALL

Robert Frost

Something there is that doesn't love a wall,
That sends the frozen-ground-swell under it
And spills the upper boulders in the sun,
And makes gaps even two can pass abreast.
The work of hunters is another thing:
I have come after them and made repair
Where they have left not one stone on a stone,
But they would have the rabbit out of hiding,
To please the yelping dogs. The gaps I mean,
No one has seen them made or heard them made,
But at spring mending-time we find them there.
I let my neighbor know beyond the hill;
And on a day we meet to walk the line
And set the wall between us once again.
We keep the wall between us as we go.
To each the boulders that have fallen to each.
And some are loaves and some so nearly balls
We have to use a spell to make them balance:
"Stay where you are until our backs our turned!"
We wear our fingers rough with handling them.
Oh, just another kind of outdoor game,
One on a side. It comes to little more:
There where it is we do not need the wall:
He is all pine and I am apple orchard.
My apple trees will never get across

And eat the cones under his pines, I tell him.
He only says, "Good fences make good neighbors."
Spring is the mischief in me, and I wonder
If I could put a notion in his head:
"*Why* do they make good neighbors? Isn't it
Where there are cows? But here there are no cows.
Before I built a wall I'd ask to know
What I was walling in or walling out,
And to whom I was like to give offense.
Something there is that doesn't love a wall,
That wants it down." I could say "Elves" to him,
But it's not elves exactly, and I'd rather
He said it for himself. I see him there,
Bringing a stone grasped firmly by the top
In each hand, like an old-stone savage armed.
He moves in darkness as it seems to me,
Not of woods only and the shade of trees.
He will not go behind his father's saying,
And he likes having thought of it so well
He says again, "Good fences make good neighbors."

THE FISH

Elizabeth Bishop

I caught a tremendous fish
and held him beside the boat
half out of water, with my hook
fast in a corner of his mouth.
He didn't fight.
He hadn't fought at all.
He hung a grunting weight,
battered and venerable
and homely. Here and there
his brown skin hung in strips
like ancient wallpaper,
and its pattern of darker brown
was like wallpaper:
shapes like full-blown roses
stained and lost through age.
He was speckled with barnacles,
fine rosettes of lime,
and infested
with tiny white sea-lice,
and underneath two or three
rags of green weed hung down.
While his gills were breathing in
the terrible oxygen
—the frightening gills,

fresh and crisp with blood,
that can cut so badly—
I thought of the coarse white flesh
packed in like feathers,
the big bones and the little bones,
the dramatic reds and blacks
of his shiny entrails,
and the pink swim-bladder
like a big peony.
I looked into his eyes
which were far larger than mine
but shallower, and yellowed,
the irises backed and packed
with tarnished tinfoil
seen through the lenses
of old scratched isinglass.
They shifted a little, but not
to return my stare.
—It was more like the tipping
of an object toward the light.
I admired his sullen face,
the mechanism of his jaw,
and then I saw
that from his lower lip

—if you could call it a lip—
grim, wet, and weaponlike,
hung five old pieces of fish-line,
or four and a wire leader
with the swivel still attached,
with all their five big hooks
grown firmly in his mouth.
A green line, frayed at the end
where he broke it, two heavier lines,
and a fine black thread
still crimped from the strain and snap
when it broke and he got away.
Like medals with their ribbons
frayed and wavering,
a five-haired beard of wisdom
trailing from his aching jaw.
I stared and stared
and victory filled up
the little rented boat,
from the pool of bilge
where oil had spread a rainbow
around the rusted engine
to the bailer rusted orange,
the sun-cracked thwarts,
the oarlocks on their strings,
the gunnels—until everything
was rainbow, rainbow, rainbow!
And I let the fish go.

ACKNOWLEDGMENTS

The Summer of the Beautiful White Horse, from MY NAME IS ARAM, by William Saroyan. Copyright © 1939, 1966 by William Saroyan. Reprinted by permission of the Trustees of Leland Stanford Junior University.

Sucker, from THE COLLECTED STORIES OF CARSON McCULLERS, by Carson McCullers. Copyright © 1978 by Flora V. Lasky, executrix of The Estate of Carson McCullers. Reprinted by permission of Houghton Mifflin Harcourt Publishing Company.

The Possibility of Evil, from JUST AN ORDINARY DAY: THE UNCOLLECTED STORIES, by Shirley Jackson. Copyright © 1965 by Stanley Edgar Hyman. Reprinted by permission of Bantam Books, a division of Random House, Inc.

Superstitions, from HOUSE OF HEROES, by Mary La Chapelle. Copyright © 1988 by Mary La Chapelle. Reprinted by permission of Crown Publishers, a division of Random House, Inc.

Gryphon, from THROUGH THE SAFETY NET, by Charles Baxter. Copyright © 1985 by Charles Baxter. Reprinted by permission of Vintage Books, a division of Random House, Inc.

Fellowship, from FRANZ KAFKA: THE COMPLETE STORIES, by Franz Kafka, edited by Nahum N. Glatzer, translated by Tania and James Stern. Copyright © 1946, 1947, 1948, 1949, 1954, 1958, 1971 by Schocken Books. Reprinted by permission of Schocken Books, a division of Random House, Inc.

Approximations, from ANYWHERE BUT HERE, by Mona Simpson. Copyright © 1986 by Mona Simpson. Reprinted by permission of Alfred A. Knopf, a division of Random House, Inc.

The Secret Lion, from THE IGUANA KILLER: TWELVE STORIES OF THE HEART, by Alberto Álvaro Ríos. Copyright © 1984 by Alberto Álvaro Ríos. Reprinted by permission of Confluence Press.

Star Food, from EMPEROR OF THE AIR, by Ethan Canin. Copyright © 1988 by Ethan Canin. Reprinted by permission of Houghton Mifflin Harcourt Publishing Company.

A Visit of Charity, from A CURTAIN OF GREEN AND OTHER STORIES, by Eudora Welty. Copyright © 1941, 1969 by Eudora Welty. Reprinted by permission of Houghton Mifflin Harcourt Publishing Company.

The Destructors, from COLLECTED STORIES OF GRAHAM GREENE, by Graham Greene. Copyright © 1954, 1982 by Graham Greene. Reprinted by permission of Viking Penguin, a division of Penguin Group (USA) Inc.

ILLUSTRATION CREDITS